JN300830

《日・英対訳／In Japanese & English》

英語落語・日本語落語で生き生き人生！
Refresh Your Life Using Rakugo!

— 大声で読んだり・陽気に笑ったり・人前で演じたり —
— Reading Aloud・Laughing Cheerfully・Performing On-Stage —

平木茂子　今井恒雄　（編・著）
Hiraki Shigeko　Imai Tsuneo　（Editor, Author）

山本正昭　竹島良憲　山田悟史　上原五百枝　根尾延子
Yamamoto Masaaki　Takeshima Yoshinori　Yamada Satoshi　Uehara Ioe　Neo Nobuko

テーラー、マーク　　マクアリア、マーク
Taylor, Mark　　McAlear, Mark

境山哲夫　上原五百枝《イラスト》
Sakaiyama Tetsuo　Uehara Ioe

TROIKA SERIES

恒星社厚生閣
Koseisha Koseikaku

本書の主人公、八つぁん・熊さんの幼年時代
The childhood of Hat-san & Kuma-san, the heroes of this book

も く じ

はじめに -- 2
Ⅰ．ここを読んだら始めよう！ -- 4
　［1］　モノにするには？ --- 4
　［2］　落語を読む（語る）際の注意 --------------------------------- 4
　［3］　登場人物紹介 --- 4
Ⅱ．《落語集》八つぁん・熊さんと落語 -------------------------------- 6
　［1］　英語、ペラペラ？ --- 6
　［2］　どっちのシャークが…… ------------------------------------- 8
　［3］　忠犬ハチ公の銅像 -- 10
　［4］　ブッシュ君の恋人 -- 16
　［5］　英会話バー -- 22
　［6］　俺は熊ではない！ -- 28
　［7］　ワッハ上方 -- 32
　［8］　我らがノラ社長 -- 36
　［9］　熊さんチの猫 -- 42
　［10］　ワンダフルジャパン --------------------------------------- 46
Ⅲ．《落語集》八つぁん・熊さんと水泳の流体力学 --------------------- 58
　［11］　新・ガールフレンド --------------------------------------- 58
　［12］　ビオンディは何故負けた？ --------------------------------- 70
　［13］　ゴーグルは何故外れる？ ----------------------------------- 82
　［14］　タイムアップはこれでバッチリ！ --------------------------- 88
　［15］　バッチャーンはダメよ！ ----------------------------------- 94
　［16］　キックの流体力学 -- 106
Ⅳ．楽しくなったらここを読もう！ ---------------------------------- 116
　［1］　落語豆知識 --- 116
　［2］　ENGLISH RAKUGO -- 120
おわりに -- 130
トロイカ・ライブラリ（平木・今井・竹島・他 著作一覧） ------------ 132
チーム紹介 -- 134

Content

Preface --- 3
I. Let's Start Rakugo Soon After Reading This Section! -------------- 5
   [1]   How to master something... ------------------------------------ 5
   [2]   Pay attention to these things when you read rakugo ----------- 5
   [3]   Introducing the main characters ------------------------------ 5
II. 《Rakugo》Hat-san・Kuma-san And Rakugo --------------------------- 7
   [1]   I Can Speak English Fluently ? ------------------------------- 7
   [2]   I Prefer The Shark In The... --------------------------------- 9
   [3]   The Statue Of A Faithful Dog, "Hachiko-" -------------------- 13
   [4]   Mr.Bush's Lover --- 19
   [5]   An English Conversation Bar --------------------------------- 25
   [6]   I'm Not A Bear! --- 30
   [7]   Rakugo Theater, "Wahha Kamigata" ---------------------------- 34
   [8]   Our Wonderful Boss, Mr.Nora --------------------------------- 39
   [9]   Kuma-san's Cat -- 44
   [10] Wonderful Japan --- 52
III. 《Rakugo》Hat-san・Kuma-san And Swimming Hydrodynamics ---------- 64
   [11] A New Girlfriend -- 64
   [12] Why Biondi Lost? -- 76
   [13] Why Goggles Come Off When Diving? --------------------------- 85
   [14] The Secret Of How To Swim Faster! --------------------------- 91
   [15] Don't Make A Big Splash! ------------------------------------ 99
   [16] Hydrodynamics Of Kicking ----------------------------------- 110
IV. Let's Read This Section If You Find Rakugo Interesting --------- 118
   [1]   What Is RAKUGO? -- 118
   [2]   ENGLISH RAKUGO --- 120
In Closing... -- 131
Troika Library (Books Written By Shigeko, Tsuneo And Yoshinori) ---- 132
Introducing The Team --- 134

さぁ、一歩、踏み出してみよう！
　　誰にでも出来て、誰にでもは出来ないけれど……。
　　　勇気を出したら、誰でも成功するから！

Let's take the first step forward!
It's possible for everyone,
and it's impossible for everyone...
But if you try, you'll succeed!

はじめに

平木 茂子（２００５年６月）
Shigeko Hiraki （2005/June）

　落語ドラマを書き始めて、大分、経ちます。
　１９９７年に、日本語だけの落語ドラマ「―八つぁん・熊さん奮闘記― 落語でわかるＯＡ化」を出版しました。昨年２００４年、これに英訳を追加し「英語落語・日本語落語大集合《日英対訳》」として出版しました。そして今年、続編の本書を出すことが出来ました。
　私は長年、大学（京都産業大学・東京家政学院筑波女子大学）で情報処理教育に携わってきました。学生への教育と同時に、中高年者向けの社会活動として、「初級プログラマ体験」や「楽しいインターネット」などの講習会を、定期的に開いてきました。
　大学で教えている間、私は、コンピュータの本質的な所や、間違いやすい所を、楽しく分かってもらえる方法はないかと考え、落語を使って説明したらどうかと思いつきました。その結果、出来上がったのが、八つぁん、熊さんがコンピュータに挑戦する落語ドラマです。その後も、八つぁん、熊さんと一緒に、ドラマを書き続けています。

　この本のテーマは「①落語に挑戦！」と「②水泳の流体力学に挑戦！」です。
　①の落語には、声を出して読んだり、暗記して人前で語ったり、自分で落語を作ったり、頭も体も……全身が生き生きとなる要素に溢れています。
　②の水泳の流体力学は、やさしく説明してあれば、水泳を知らない人にも楽しく理解出来ます。
　これらを通して、「新しいことに挑戦することの楽しさ」を知っていただけたら、嬉しく思います。

Preface

Shigeko Hiraki

Over 10 years have passed since I started to write rakugo drama.

My first rakugo drama book was published in 1997 under the title, "Hat-san and Kuma-san try to learn a computer!", though it was written in Japanese only. Last year, 2004, I translated it into English, and the new book, "A Big Selection Of Rakugo In English And Japanese!" was published. This year I wrote this book as the sequel to it.

For a long time, I was teaching Computer Science as a Professor at two universities, (Kyoto Sangyo Univ. and Tokyo Kasei Gakuin Tsukuba Women's Univ.). At the same time I was holding workshops for middle-aged citizens on, "Let's experience being a computer programmer!" and "Let's enjoy the internet!" and so on.

While teaching at univ., I was thinking about what was the best way for understanding the most difficult parts of the computer. Finally I thought of a very good way. I should explain them using rakugo and hence I wrote my first rakugo drama book. In it, two young non-educated guys, Hat-san and Kuma-san, try to master the computer. Since then, I've continued to write rakugo drama with Hat-san and Kuma-san.

The themes of this book are ① "Let's try to perform rakugo!" and ② "Let's try to learn swimming hydrodynamics!"

① You can use rakugo for reading aloud, performing in front of an audience and writing rakugo by yourself. These are the elements for refreshing our health (body and soul).

② About swimming hydrodynamics, even non-swimmers can understand it if it's written easily such as in this book.

I hope trying either of the two helps you to find a fun way to learn new and unknown challenges!

Ⅰ．ここを読んだら始めよう！

平木 茂子（Shigeko Hiraki）

[1] モノにするには？
　スポーツでも芸事でもその他、何でも、まずは体で覚える・実践から入るのがモノにする近道です。次に、簡単なことをイヤと言うほど繰り返す。これが出来る人なら必ず成功します。難しい理屈はヌキにして、とにかく声を出して落語を読んでみましょう。何度も練習しているうちに楽しさや興味を感じたら、「Ⅳ．楽しくなったらここを読もう！」を読んでみてください。

[2] 落語を読む（語る）際の注意
　1．大きな声で、間（マ）をとりながら、ゆっくり読んでください。
　　★　カンマの後では、一呼吸してください。
　　★　ピリオドの後では、二呼吸してください。
　　★　この記号（？　！　……。　...）の後では三呼吸してください。
　僅かこれだけで、玄人の読み方に近づきます。もしカンマの箇所を増やした方が読みやすければ、いくらでも追加してください。
　2．下の箇所は読みません。
　　★　角ガッコ（【　】　[　]）に囲まれた部分。（例：【熊】　[3]）
　　★　右端の /100 とか /500 などの連番。

[3] 登場人物紹介
①　頑張る熊さん：家庭の事情で中学しか出ていない。ノラ社の社員。
②　そそっかしい八つぁん：同じく中卒。熊さんの親友。ノラ社の社員。
③　我らのノラ社長：こんな社長にいて欲しい！
④　優しいおっかぁ：熊さんの母親。夫、亡き後、二人の子供を育てあげる。
⑤　可愛い千代さん：熊さんの愛妻。熊さんのことを、とても尊敬してる。
⑥　いたずらトラ助＆可愛いクルミ：熊さんの子供。
⑦　元気なマリちゃん：誰にも負けない８８歳！
⑧　美人のゆきちゃん：スナック「ゆき」のママ。
⑨　カッコいいＴコーチ＆Ｙコーチ：水泳の流体力学の専門家。
⑩　猫のファイル：熊さんチの軒下に捨てられていたのを助けられた「忠猫」。

I. Let's Start Rakugo Soon After Reading This Section!

Shigeko Hiraki

[1] How to master something...

If you want to improve something, for example playing sports, musical instruments, learning languages and so on, you're better to start first from practice, not from theory or study. Next, you should practice as much as you can. If you can do this, you'll surely succeed. If you find this interesting, read, "IV. Let's Read This Section If You Find Rakugo Interesting".

[2] Pay attention to these things when you read rakugo
 1. Read rakugo loudly and take a pause as shown below.
  ★ After a comma, take a one-breath-pause.
  ★ After a period or full-stop, take a two-breath-pause.
  ★ After these symbols (? ! ……。 ...) take a three-breath-pause.
 If you keep to these rules, your reading will improve. If you want to add periods, put them anywhere.
 2. Don't read the following parts.
  ★ The parts surounded by "【 】 [ ]". (nb.【K】[3])
  ★ The sequence number on the right side. (nb. /100 /500)

[3] Introducing the main characters
① Fighting Kuma-san : Junior high grad. A worker at Nora Co..
② Hasty Hat-san : Junior high grad. A worker at Nora Co..
③ Our Boss Nora : The ideal boss!
④ Tender Mom : Kuma-san's Mother. Raised her children alone.
⑤ Lovable Chiyo-san : Kuma-san's wife. Respects Kuma-san a lot.
⑥ Naughty Torasuke & cuty Kurumi : Kuma-san's children.
⑦ Fresh Mari-chan : 88 years old, but unyielding!
⑧ Pretty Yuki-chan : The owner of the snack bar, "Yuki".
⑨ Cool T-coach & Y-coach : Specialists in swimming hydrodynamics.
⑩ File (cat) : Dumped on Kuma-san's doorstep. A faithful cat!

II.《落語集》八つぁん・熊さんと落語

[1] 英語、ペラペラ？

〔根尾 延子（Nobuko Neo）〕

　大企業で、バリバリの営業マンとして活躍してきたＹさんは、定年後の今も元気いっぱいで、英会話に熱中しています。先週、私の通う落語教室（HOEインターナショナル）に、高座での落語の演じ方を学ぶためやって来ました。

～～～～～～～～～～～～～～～～～～～～～～～～～～～～～～～～～

【Y】やー、Ｎちゃん、元気だったかい？　英語は、少しはマシになったかい？
【N】私はさっぱりよ。Ｙさんは？
【Y】ま、外人さんには、楽に話しかけられるようになったので、次は、宴会で英語落語をやってみようと思っているんだ。
【N】凄いわー、Ｙさん！　アッと言う間にペラペラになったのね。
【Y】ま、それ程でもないけどさ。でも来週、俺の通っている英語教室の先生が帰国するので、そのサヨナラ・パーティで、披露するんだよ。
【N】まぁ、素晴らしいじゃないの！　頑張ってね、Ｙさん！

～～～～～～～～～～～～～～～～～～～～～～～～～～～～～～～～～

【N】Ｙさん、おはよー。サヨナラ・パーティでの落語は、どうだった？
【Y】ウン……。他の連中の英語力が低くてね、俺が何を喋っているのか理解出来ず、キョトンとして、俺を見ていただけなんだよ。
【N】まぁ、失礼しちゃうわね。でも、先生は、褒めてくれたんでしょ。
【Y】先公のヤツ、俺にこう言ったんだぜ、「Ｙさん、他の言語を学ぶのも良いけれど、これからは英語も勉強しましょうね」だなんてさ。アイツまで、程度が低いんだ。参った、参った……。

---- 【終り】 ----

II. 《Rakugo》Hat-san・Kuma-san And Rakugo

[1] I Can Speak English Fluently ?

〔Nobuko Neo〕

Mr.Y worked very hard for a big company as an ace salesman. After retirement he is eager to learn speak English. Last week, he came to my rakugo class, HOE International to learn how to perform rakugo in English on-stage.

~~~~~~

【Y】Hi, Nobuko! How are you? How is your English? You've made a lot of progress, haven't you?
【N】Not yet. How about you?
【Y】Now I can speak to foreigners easily. Next, I'll try to perform my rakugo in English at a party.
【N】Great! You already speak fluent English!
【Y】Thanks a lot for your compliment! By the way, next week we'll have a farewell party for our English teacher, and I'll perform my rakugo in English there.
【N】Oh, that's a good idea! Good luck, Mr.Y!

~~~~~~

【N】Hi, Mr.Y! Good morning! How was your rakugo performance at the farewell party?
【Y】Well... I'm vert disappointed because the other students' conversational skills were so bad. Not a single student could understand what I was saying.
【N】Oh, that's too bad... But... your English teacher praised you, didn't she?
【Y】Oh, the teacher said to me, "Mr.Y, you could learn any other language but first you should learn English I hope..." I'm sure her conversational skill was also very low too...

---- 【END】 ----

[2] どっちのシャークが……

〔平木 茂子 (Shigeko Hiraki)〕

---------------------（オーストラリアの休日）----------------------
- 【熊】八つぁん、一体、どうしたんだい？　冴えない顔、しちゃってさ。
- 【八】熊さん、実はな、家でナニと、ちょっと……。
- 【熊】何だか分かんないけど……とにかく、少し泳がないかい？　元気になるぜ。
- 【八】そうだな。でも、俺、海で泳ぐの、始めてなんだ。
----------（ザブーン！　八つぁんと熊さん、飛び込む）------------
- 【熊】どうだい、気持ち、いいだろ。さぁ、あっちまで泳ごうぜ。
- 【八】ウン。こりゃ、熊さんの言う通り、いい気分だ。あれれ……ありゃ何だい？　シャークの背鰭（ゼビレ）じゃ……。
- 【熊】八つぁん、泳いでいても、大丈夫なんだよ。
- 【八】それ、どういう意味だい？　シャークだぜ！　俺、餌食になんぞ、なりたくないよ。逃げよう！
- 【熊】そうそう、言うの忘れてた。
- 【八】何をだい、熊さん？
- 【熊】あすこに、シャークが入れないように、鉄の柵がしてあるんだよ。だから、泳いでいても大丈夫なんだ。
- 【八】そうは言っても……キャー、凄いヤツが近づいて来たぞー。でもな、俺、ウチのシャークより、こっちの方が、まだいいや……。

---- 【終り】 ----

【註：オチの部分は、英語と日本語では変えています。】

[2] I Prefer The Shark In The...　　　　　　　　　　　　/100

[Mark Taylor]

------------------ (Holidays in Australia) -------------------- /110
【K】Hey Hat-san! Why are you looking so sad?　　　　　/120
【H】Ohhh, I have had some troubles at home.　　　　　　/130
【K】Well, come and have a swim. It will cheer you up and /140
you'll feel better.
【H】Okay. But this is the first time I've swum in an ocean pool. /150
----- (Splosh! Hat-san & Kuma-san dive into the ocean pool) ------ /160
【K】It's fresh, isn't it! Let's swim to the other end.　　/170
【H】Okay. This is great. You're right, Kuma-san. But what's /180
that?! I can see a shark fin?
【K】Keep on swimming! It's no problem.　　　　　　　/190
【H】What do you mean? It's a shark! I don't want to be /200
shark meat! I'm getting out!
【K】Oh, I understand I forgot to tell you.　　　　　　　/210
【H】What?　　　　　　　　　　　　　　　　　　　　/220
【K】There's a steel fence under the water that separates /230
the pool from the Ocean.
【H】That shark is getting closer! Swimming with the sharks /240
at home sounds better to me! Bye Bye!

---- 【END】----

[3] 忠犬ハチ公の銅像　　　　　　　　　　　　　　　　　/100

〔平木　茂子（Shigeko Hiraki）〕

　八つぁんと熊さんは、4月から大阪に転勤になりました。ノラ社長が、　/110
2人を大阪で修行させようと、考えたからです。
　大阪に赴任した二人は、半年ほど前から始めていた水泳を続けるため、
近くのプールに入会しました。そこで二人は「英語落語教室・門下生募集
・HOEインターナショナル」のポスターを見つけました。新しいことが
大好きな八つぁんと熊さんは、早速、入門しました。
　さぁ、二人の、大阪での仕事と水泳と英語落語の毎日が始まります。
~~~~~~~~~~~~~~~~~~~~~~~~~~~~~~~~~~~~~~
　【熊】八つぁん、先週の、英語で落語の教室は、楽しかったなぁ。　　　/120
　【八】ウン。俺達、初めての参加だったのに、高座に上がって、キチンと　/130
教えてもらってさ、サイコーだったじゃないか。
　【熊】これからも、時間の都合がつく限り、参加させてもらおうよ。　　/140
　【八】そうしよう。　　　　　　　　　　　　　　　　　　　　　　　　/150
　【熊】でも、八つぁん、次の時は、何か準備していかないと……。　　　/160
　【八】そうなんだ。そうしないと、ついていけないと思うよ。　　　　　/170
　【熊】俺は、こないだ習った「植木屋」が簡単だから、アレを暗記してい　/180
こうと思うんだけど、八つぁんは何にする？
　【八】ウーン、俺は創作落語をやりたいんだ。つまり、熊さんが作って、　/190
俺がそれを語るってのをさ……。
　【熊】えっ、何で、俺が、八つぁんのために書くんだよ。自分で書けば、　/200
いいじゃないか。
　【八】熊さんよ、これは、俺達のガキの頃からの、役割分担じゃないか。　/210
熊さんが頭を使い、俺が体を使うってのはさー。そうだろ？
　【熊】もう……。　　　　　　　　　　　　　　　　　　　　　　　　　/220
　【八】じゃ、書いてくれるな。　　　　　　　　　　　　　　　　　　　/230
　【熊】八つぁんたら……いいかい、落語って、最後にオチをつけないと、　/240
いけないんだぜ。それは難しくて、俺にはムリなんだよ。
　【八】だったら、今回は、「オチの無い落語」でいいからさ。　　　　　/250
　【熊】オチの無い落語？　八つぁん、それ、どういう落語なんだい？　　/260
　【八】言葉通り、オチをつけないのさ。　　　　　　　　　　　　　　　/270

【熊】それじゃ、落語に、ならないと思うけど。　　　　　　　　　　/280
【八】いいじゃないか。初めのうちは、ちゃんと出来なくて当たり前だも　/290
の。作っているうちに上手になるさ、熊さんなら。だから、書いてくれよ。
【熊】八つぁんたら……。　　　　　　　　　　　　　　　　　　　/300
【八】そうそう、それと話の内容は、でっきるだけ短く・簡単で・やさし　/310
いのを頼むよ。高座で、俺、立ち往生……じゃない、座り往生したくない
んだよ。なにしろ、俺って気が弱いだろ、すぐビクビクしちゃうんだよ。
【熊】八つぁんが、いつ・どこで、ビクビクしたんだよ。ズーズーしい。　/320
【八】ま、とにかく、明日の昼休みまでに、考えといてくれよ、熊さん。　/330
-------------------（さーて、翌日の昼休み）---------------------/340
【八】どうだい、熊さん、八公にぴったりの落語、出来たかい？　　　/350
【熊】出来たことは、出来たけど、でも、オチがな、イマ・イチなんだ。　/360
【八】いいんだったら、そんなこと。ところで話は、短く・簡単で・やさ　/370
しくなってるんだろうな。そこだけが心配だぜ。よーし、早速、練習する
から、教えてくれ。
【熊】ＯＫ。いいか八つぁん、この食堂のテーブルを高座と思って、そこ　/380
に上がれ。よし、それから、自分の名を名乗って、頭を下げろ。
【八】荒木八太郎、八つぁんでーす！　　　　　　　　　　　　　　/390
【熊】よし。次に、手を前につけ。　　　　　　　　　　　　　　　/400
【八】こうかい？　　　　　　　　　　　　　　　　　　　　　　　/410
【熊】ま、そんなとこだ。次に、その　　　　　　　　　　　　　　/420
ままの姿勢で、顔を上に向けろ。よし、
そこで、目を大きく開けて空を見ろ。
そのまま１分、絶対に動くな。
【八】熊さん、ここまでは大丈夫だ！　　　　　　　　　　　　　　/430
問題はこっからだな。それで、次は、
何を話せばいいんだい。
【熊】これで、しまいだ。　　　　　　　　　　　　　　　　　　　/440
【八】えっ、まだ、何も話しちゃいないぜ。　　　　　　　　　　　/450
【熊】こう言えばいいんだ。「以上で、東京・渋谷駅前の銅像、忠犬ハチ　/460
公の話を終わります。ハチ公は、私の生まれるずーっと前に、死んでしま
ったので、私にはこれ以上、何もお伝えすることがなくて、とっても残念
です」ってな。

----【終り】----

《忠犬ハチ公のこと》

　東京・渋谷駅前に大きな犬の銅像が立っています。忠犬ハチ公の像です。
　ハチ公は、１９２３年生まれの牡の純粋秋田犬です。東京大学教授の上野博士が生まれたばかりのハチ公の主人となりました。博士は、この犬を大層可愛がりました。
　やがて、ハチ公は、渋谷駅まで博士の送り迎えをするようになりました。ところが１９２５年の５月、ハチ公に送られて大学に向かった博士は、そのまま帰らぬ人となりました。
　その後も、博士を出迎え続けるハチ公の姿に人々は感動し、１９３４年に銅像が立てられました。その翌年、１９３５年、ハチ公は亡くなりました。

[3] The Statue Of A Faithful Dog, "Hachiko-"

[Shigeko Hiraki]

Hat-san and Kuma-san were transferred to the Osaka branch from the Tokyo main office this April. Their boss, Mr. Nora, thought that they needed higher training at a distant place.

As soon as they moved to Osaka, they found a good swimming pool and became members there. They started swimming six months ago and now they are eager to swim more. At the swimming pool, they found a poster on what was written, "Welcome to our rakugo in English class! (HOE International in Osaka)". As they are fond of trying new things, they joined the rakugo class.

A fresh life in Osaka with new jobs, swimmimg, and rakugo in English has now started for Hat-san and Kuma-san.

~~~~~~

【K】Hat-san, we had such a great time at last week's rakugo class in English at HOE, didn't we?

【H】Yeah, we did rakugo in English for the first time. We were sitting on a small stage and the teachers taught us how to speak and perform rakugo. It was so exciting!

【K】I'd like to take as many lessons as possible there.

【H】Me, too.

【K】And... I think we should prepare... I mean memorize some rakugo before the next lesson.

【H】Right. Without preparation we'll drop out.

【K】I intend to memorize the story, "The Florist" that we learnt last time. It's short and easy. How about you, Hat-san?

【H】Well... I want to perform an original rakugo that Kuma-san will hopefully write for me.

【K】What? I'm gonna write rakugo for you? Why don't you write it yourself?

【H】Kuma-san, you use your brain and I use my body. We've always done it like this ever since our childhood. Haven't we?

【K】Hat-san... you... /220
【H】So, I'm asking you to write an original one for me... /230
【K】Oh Hat-san, you're so cheeky! As you know rakugo must /240
have a punch line (ochi) at the end. I can't write a punch
line because it's very difficult.
【H】OK, OK. Then this time write rakugo without a punch line. /250
【K】What? What's rakugo without a punch line like, Hat-san? /260
【H】As I said, it's rakugo which has no punch line. /270
【K】It's not rakugo... is it? /280
【H】Don't worry about that, Kuma-san. Writing rakugo is /290
difficult for you now, but you'll become better and better
as you write rakugo many times. So, write one for me!
【K】Hat-san... /300
【H】And... as you know, I'm shy, so I'm always nervous on-stage. /310
So, please try to write a short, simple and easy story.
【K】Hat-san, I've never seen you so nervous. /320
【H】Is that so? Anyway, write some rakugo for me by tomorrow /330
at lunch time.
----------------- (Lunch time the next day) -------------------- /340
【H】Hey, Kuma-san, have you written any rakugo for me? /350
【K】I've written it but the punch line's not good... /360
【H】Oh, don't worry about that, Kuma-san. All I need is rakugo /370
that's short, simple and easy. OK, I want to practice it right
now. Tell me how to perform your rakugo.
【K】Well, Hat-san, imagine this table is a small stage. /380
Sit on it. OK! Next, say your name and bow.
【H】My name is Hachitaro- Araki. Call me Hat-san! /390
【K】OK. Next, put your hands down on the ground. /400
【H】Like this? /410
【K】Yeah. OK. Next, lift your chin up a little, open your /420
eyes wide, look at the sky and keep your body motionless
for a whole minute. Don't move a muscle.
【H】Hey, Kuma-san, I can do everything so far! Then the story /430
starts, I suppose. Well, what do I have to say?

【K】 Nothing. That's your rakugo.

【H】 What? I haven't said anything.

【K】 OK, Just say. This is my rakugo about a faithful dog called "Hachiko-". He's now looking at us as a statue at Shibuya station in Tokyo. Hachiko- died before I was born, so I know nothing about him. Oh, I'm very, very sorry I can't tell you any more about him...

---- 【END】 ----

《About A Faithful Dog, "Hachiko-"》

  In front of Shibuya station in Tokyo stands a statue on which is written "A Faithful Dog, Hachiko-".

  Hachiko-, a male, Japanese "Akita" dog, was born in 1923. The master was Dr.Ueno, a Professor of Tokyo University, loved Hachiko- very much.

  Everyday Hachiko- walked with his master to the Shibuya station and then returned home by himself. But, on 21st May, 1925, after Hachiko- saw off Dr.Ueno at the station, the doctor never returned.

  After that, Hachiko- continued to go to the station to meet him. People felt very sorry for Hachiko- and they built a statue for him in 1934, the year before Hachiko-'s death.

[4] ブッシュ君の恋人

〔平木 茂子 (Shigeko Hiraki)〕

【八】熊さん、今度の忘年会でやる余興のことだけど、俺達は、ＨＯＥの落語教室で覚えた英語落語をやってみるってのは、どうだろう？

【熊】そうか、俺達には英語落語って秘密兵器があったな。あれなら珍しいから、皆、びっくりするだろうな。そうしよう。俺達、もう、5つぐらい覚えたから、その中から選べばいいんだ。それで、八つぁんは、どれがいいって思うかい？

【八】俺は、「台湾猿」が好きだけど、熊さんは？

【熊】全部、面白いから迷っちゃうなぁ。勿論、俺も、それは好きだよ。そうだな、そしたら、「台湾猿」に決めるか。それじゃ、今日から仕事が終わったら練習を始めようぜ。

【八】熊さん、どうせやるんなら、こうしたら、どうだろう。「台湾猿」の猿を、ほかの動物に変えて、やってみるってのは？

【熊】えっ、俺達にそんなこと出来るかなぁ。だって、変える部分は俺達で考えなくちゃいけないんだろ。それに、オチも、変えなくちゃいけないから……難しくないかなぁ……。

【八】難しいから勉強になるんじゃないかい。俺達は、初心者なんだから、「オチの無い落語」でも、かまわないと思うよ。

【熊】八つぁんの言う通りだな。それで、猿を何に変えるんだい？

【八】馬に変えたら、どうかと思うんだ。

【熊】馬？ 犬や猫じゃないのかい。馬とはびっくりだなぁ。だけどさ、八つぁん、馬で、うまく話が作れそうかい？

【八】俺、ひらめいたんだよ。それ、喋ってみるから、いつものように、熊さんがそれを書き留めて、後で、ちゃんとまとめてくれるかい？

【熊】分かった。エンピツと紙は、ここにあるから、始めていいよ。

【八】それじゃ、ペット・ショップに来た客が、「何かペットになるような珍しい動物はないか？」って聞くところまでは「台湾猿」と同じだから、その続きをやるぜ。

～～～～～～～～～～～～～～～～～～～～～～～～～～～～～～

【主】お客さま、この店には世界各国の馬、それも、ちゃんと調教された馬を、色々と、取りそろえてございます。

【客】ほぅ、近頃は、馬も、ペットとして売られているのか。
【主】さようでございます。お客さまのようなエリートの方は、ペットとして、馬はいかがでしょうか。
【客】フーン。馬といっても顔も姿も様々のようだが、この白い美しい馬は、どこから来て、何という名前だ？
【主】カナダから来ました。メス馬の、メープル・シロップでございます。
【客】その隣は？
【主】ロシヤから来ましたマッシュルーム、その隣が中国のチャーハンで、その隣がタイのトム・ヤム・クンで、ございます。
【客】何だか、食い物の名前ばかりのようだが。
【主】いえいえ、そうではございません。向かいの小屋の左から、ギリシャから来ましたソクラテス、その横がイギリスのエリザベス、あ、これは、大分、年をとっております、そしてその横が日本生まれの、ゴジラ・マツイでございます。
【客】向こうの離れた小屋で、大暴れしている馬は、どこ産だ？
【主】あ、あれは、アメリカ西部から参りました。他人を、いや、他馬を攻撃するのが大好きな馬でございます。危険なので、隔離〔かくり〕しております。
【客】名は、何と言うんだ。
【主】ブッシュでございます。
【客】名前も、凄味があるなぁ。しかし、俺も、世界の一流人の仲間入りをしたいと思っているからには、ブッシュぐらいを、家来〔けらい〕にせんとな。よーし、ブッシュを買うことに決めたぞ。
【主】あ、ありがとう・ございま〜す！
---------------（１ヵ月後、同じペットショップで）----------------
【客】おい、おやじ、あのブッシュだけど、ウチに来て以来、元気がなくてな、暴れるどころか食欲もないんだよ。
【主】それは……獣医に、見せた方がよろしいかと……。
【客】無論、獣医にも見せたのだが、それでも、さっぱり分からんのだ。そこで、ワシは、散々、考えて、ようやく今朝、原因をつきとめたんだ。
【主】どういうことで、ございますか。
【客】ワシがブッシュを、あのカナダから来た美人……じゃなくて美馬だがな、アレと引き離したのが原因なんだ。だからあのメスを買って、ヤツに当てがってやろうと思うんだ。まだ、あのメスは売れ残っているかい？

【主】お客さま、有難いお言葉ですが、私には、ブッシュが、恋わずらい　/450
とはとても思えませんが。さーて、どうしたものか……。あっ、そうです、
そうです、良い考えがございます。実は私ども、裏の倉庫に物凄いヤツを
隠しておりますが、それをお買い求めいただければ、即座に、問題解決、
いや、前以上にファイト満々になること、請け合いでございます。おーい、
誰か、オサマ・ビン・ラディンをここに連れて来て、お見せしなさーい！

----【終り】----

[4] Mr.Bush's Lover

[Shigeko Hiraki]

【H】 Kuma-san, I have an idea for our performance at the end of year party. Because we're learning to do rakugo in English at HOE, shall we perform some rakugo at the party?

【K】 Sure! We can amaze everyone with our secret weapon, rakugo in English! Now we know more than five stories, so let's pick one of those. But which one's the best for the party? Hat-san, what's your favorite one?

【H】 My favorite is the "Monkey from Taiwan". What's yours?

【K】 They're all interesting, it's difficult to choose one... but I like "The monkey from Taiwan" too... OK, let's perform that one at the party. Let's start practicing it today after work.

【H】 Kuma-san, what do you think about this idea; we could change the "monkey" to another animal.

【K】 What? Could we do something so hard? We would have to write the last part ourselves... and we would have to think of a punch line (ochi)... It's too difficult...

【H】 Of course it's difficult, but it's very good practice for us too. We're beginners, so I think it's OK if our rakugo doesn't have a punch line.

【K】 You're absolutely right, Hat-san. Well, what animal do you want to change it to?

【H】 I want to change the monkey to a horse.

【K】 Wow! A horse! I imagined a dog or a cat... I'm really surprised... Well, Hat-san, can you make a story about a horse?

【H】 I've got it! Kuma-san, I'll tell you my idea now. Write it down and then you can make a good rakugo with it later, OK?

【K】 OK. I have a pen and paper. Go for it.

【H】 Well, the first half of the rakugo is the same, like this; /230
a customer goes to a pet shop and asks, "Do you have any rare
animals?" Then I'll continue it in a different way.

~~~~~~

【M】 Welcome to my shop! I have a lot of rare animals here! /240

【C】 Well, well... Do you sell horses as pets nowadays? /250

【M】 Yes, sir. I recommend a horse to a sophisticated customer /260
like you. How about a well-trained horse as your pet? I have
horses from all over the world.

【C】 Oh, some horses are handsome, some seem clever and some /270
are old... What's the name of that beautiful white one?

【M】 It's a Canadian horse. It's female and her name is /280
Maple Syrup.

【C】 And the next one? /290

【M】 It's from Russia and its name is Mushroom. The next is /300
from China, its name is Fried Rice. The next is from Thailand
and its name is Tom-Yam-Kum.

【C】 So they're all named after food? /310

【M】 No, no, not all of them. In the next stable, from left to /320
right, we have Socrates from Greece, Elizabeth from England, oh,
she's old, and finally a Japanese horse called Godzilla Matsui.

【C】 What about that horse going crazy in the separate stable? /330

【M】 He came over from the Wild West of Texas. He loves wars. /340
As he's very dangerous, I keep him away from the other horses.

【C】 What's his name? /350

【M】 His name's Bush. /360

【C】 Oh, even the name's terrible... But I want to become /370
a very famous man all over the world, so I must ride on
an aggressive horse like Bush. OK, I'll buy Bush.

【M】 Oh, thank you very much, sir. /380

--------------- (At the same shop, 1 month later) --------------- /390

【C】 Hey buddy, that Bush you sold me has no energy, /400
he's not aggressive and he won't eat anything since he came to
my house.

【M】 I think you'd better call a vet... /410
【C】 I did already. But, even the vet didn't know what's /420
wrong with Bush. I was thinking about it and this morning
I figured out why he has no energy.
【M】 Oh, why? /430
【C】 The reason is this; I separated Bush from his lover, /440
the Canadian beauty. So I'm here today to buy that Canadian
horse for Bush. Do you still have her for sale here?
【M】 Oh, sir, thank you for coming back... But I never /450
thought Bush would fall in love... Well, what shall I do?...
Oh, I have a good idea! I have one secret horse. I hide him
in my shelter. If you buy that horse, all of the problems
will be sorted out at once. Hey! Bring Osama Bin Laden here...

---- 【END】 ----

[5] 英会話バー

〔平木 茂子（Shigeko Hiraki）〕

【八】熊さん、ビッグ・ニュースだ！ ビッグ・ニュースだ！ 聞いて、驚くな。

【熊】又々、八つぁんのビッグ・ニュースが始まった。どうせ、だれだれちゃんが、今日、はいているミニスカートは最高だぜ……とかだろ。

【八】何、言ってるんだよ。そんなレベルの低い話じゃないんだよ。ホレ、駅のそばにビルが建築中だっただろ。あれ、英会話バーなんだって。今日がオープン初日だそうだよ。今晩、行ってみないかい。

【熊】そうかー、仕事の後で英会話の勉強に行ってるって言えば、聞こえがいいなぁ。

【八】ウン。いい店が出来てよかったよ。とにかく、名前がいいだろ。

------------------（さーて、その夜、英会話バーで）------------------

【熊】八つぁん、入口に「この注意書きをよく読んで、お入りください」って書いてあるよ。ナニナニ……「注意１：お１人様、ビール１杯つき、２千円で、何時間でもご利用いただけます！」だってさ。安いなぁ。

【八】熊さん、外人のかわい子ちゃん達の写真の横に、こう書いてあるよ。「注意２：アタシ達と、英語で楽しくお喋りしましょーね。特に初心者の方は、来てね！」だってさ。ワーイ！

【熊】八つぁん、こうも書いてあるけど。「注意３：お帰りまでに、１回は舞台に上がって、英語で何かやってください。歌でも、詩の朗読でも、自己紹介でも、何でもOKです。なお、舞台の上では、英語だけをお使いください。もし、日本語を使った場合は、１単語につき、百円、いただきます」だってさ。俺達、大丈夫かなぁ……。

【八】熊さん、そりゃ、心配ないよ。だって俺達は、HOEで習った英語落語を、そのままやるんだからさ。

【熊】八つぁん、ここに、嬉しいことが、書いてあるぜ。「注意４：もし舞台で、日本語を一切、使わなかった場合は、サービス券を差し上げます。その券で、かわい子ちゃんと、カクテルをお楽しみください」だってさ。

【八】ウワー！ こりゃ、今夜は豪勢になるな。１回、舞台に上がれば、可愛い子ちゃんとカクテルか。俺は、４回はいけるな。いいぜ、いいぜ、よーし、中に入ろうぜ。

> いよいよ、八つぁん・熊さんが、舞台に上がる時がきました。
> 店のマネージャーが、英語で2人を紹介します。

【マ】次は、八つぁん、熊さんの、英語落語です。どちらが、先にやりますか。八つぁんですか、それとも、熊さんですか？
(Next performance is a rakugo in English by Hat-san and Kuma-san. OK guys, who's first? Hat-san or Kuma-san?)

【熊】おいおい、八つぁん、俺達の番のようだぜ。どっちが先かを、聞いているようだが、八つぁん、先にやるかい？

【八】熊さん、俺、何だかおっかなくって……熊さん、先にやってくれよ。

【熊】八つぁんとしたことが、どうしたんだよ？　それじゃ、俺が、先にやるけど、俺が「植木屋」で、八つぁんが「台湾猿」で、いいんだな。

【八】ウン……。

【熊】そんじゃ、俺、いっちょやってくるぜ。《トコ・トコ・トコ……》
私の名前は、熊さんです。落語の題は、植木屋です。おい植木屋。いらっしゃいませ。お前の所には、どんな種類の花でもあるか……。
(My name is Kuma-san. The title of my rakugo is "The Florist". Hey, Florist! May I help you? Do you have all kinds of flower?...)

> さーて、熊さんは、無事、話し終わりました。店の人達の拍手を浴び
> サービス券ももらった熊さんは、大喜びです。

【熊】さぁ、八つぁん、お前の番だぜ。頑張ってこいよ。

【八】熊さん、俺、何だか、おっかなくって、止めるってワケには……。

【熊】今更、何いってるんだよ。いけーったら……。

> 熊さんに、背中をドーンと押された八つぁんは、その勢いで
> 《タッ・タッ・タッ》と、舞台に押し出されました。

【八】オッ、オッ、オッ、俺は、ハッ、ハッ、ハッ、八つぁんです。あっ、いけねぇ、日本語を使っちゃったよ。英語・英語と。
My name is /えーと/ Hat-san. I'm going to do /えーと, なんだっけ, そうだ/ rakugo too. The title is /えーと/ Monkey from Taiwan.

> すっかり、あがってしまった八つぁんは、舞台で日本語を
> 使ってしまい、マネージャーに、英語でこう言われてしまいました。

【マ】八つぁん、貴方は、今、１０回、日本語を、使いましたね。千円、頂きます。残念ながら、可愛い子ちゃんとの、カクテルでのカンパイは、ありません。
(Hat-san, you said 10 Japanese words. That's 1000 yen. Pay up!
And you've lost your chance to have a drink with a cute girl!)

【八】あー、俺、大失敗しちゃったよー。マネージャーさん、もう一度、やり直しさせて、くれないかい？

> 又々、八つぁんは、マネージャーに英語で言われてしまいました。

【マ】おー、八つぁん、貴方は、今、８つの、日本語を使いましたね。合計、千八百円、頂きます。
(Oh, Hat-san, you said another 8 Japanese words. That's 1800 yen!)

---- 【終り】 ----

[5] An English Conversation Bar

[Shigeko Hiraki]

【H】Hey Kuma-san, big news, big news!... You'll be surprised when you hear it!

【K】Hat-san, we're never surprised by your "big news". It's always a story like, "That girl's wearing a very nice miniskirt."

【H】Oh, today's news isn't dirty. You know they're building something near the station. It's a bar, but not a regular bar. It's an English conversation bar! It sounds great! Let's go there tonight!

【K】It sounds good if I can go and learn English conversation after work.

【H】Yeah, it sounds like a really good chance for us.

-------------------- (That night, at the bar) ------------------

【K】Hey Hat-san, look at this notice... "Please enter after reading the following. (No.1) You can stay and enjoy this bar for as long as you want for just 2000 yen including one free glass of beer. Wow, it's cheap!

【H】Kuma-san, here's another thing. (No.2) Come and have a nice chat with us in English! Beginners are especially welcome! And here are the staff photos! Oh, they're all non-Japanese. They're so good looking!

【K】Hat-san, look. (No.3) You must do something on-stage in English. Any performance is OK, such as singing a song, reading a poem or introducing yourself. The important thing is this. If you speak Japanese on-stage, you must pay 100 yen for each word. Oh, Hat-san, I think we'll have to pay a lot...

【H】Kuma-san, don't worry about it. We'll each do rakugo we learned at HOE.

【K】Hat-san, look at this. (No.4) If you don't speak a single word of Japanese on-stage, we'll give you a ticket for a free drink. You can use it to have a free cocktail with a cute girl.

【H】 Wow! We're gonna have such a good night tonight! /220
One free cocktail for one performance! I'll get four free
cocktails with four cute girls tonight! OK Kuma-san, let's
go into the bar!

> Now it's time for Hat-san and Kuma-san to go on-stage. /230
> The manager calls them up and introduces them in English.

【Manager】 The next performance is rakugo by Hat-san and /240
Kuma-san. OK guys, who's first? Hat-san or Kuma-san?
【K】 Hey Hat-san, I think he means... he's asking who's gonna /250
go first... I think it's better if you go first...
【H】 I'm afraid... Kuma-san, you go first... /260
【K】 What's the matter with you, Hat-san? OK, I'll go first. /270
But I'm gonna do "The Florist", and you're gonna do "The monkey
from Taiwan", OK?
【H】 OK... /280
【K】 Well, here I go... My name is Kumasuke. The title of my /290
rakugo is "The Florist"... "Hey Florist! May I help you?
Do you have all kinds of flowers?...".

> Kuma-san does the story very well and everyone claps. /300
> Kuma-san is very happy and receives a cocktail ticket.

【K】 Hey Hat-san, now it's your turn. Good luck! /310
【H】 Kuma-san, I can't do my story... /320
【K】 Hey, what are you talking about? Go for it! /330

> Kuma-san pushes Hat-san onto the stage. /340

【H】 O-O-O-OREWA, /HA-HA-HACHITARO-/DESU. /A-, IKENE-/NIHONGO O/ /350
TSUKACCHATTAYO. /EIGO, EIGO TO.../
(My name is Hat-san... Oh, I'm speaking Japanese. I must speak
only English...)

| Hat-san is too excited and he uses some Japanese words. After his story, the Manager has a chat with him... | /360 |

【Manager】Hat-san, you said 10 Japanese words. That's 1000 yen. Pay up! And you've lost your chance to have a drink with a cute girl! /370

【H】A-/ORE, /DAISHIPPAI/SHICHATTAYO. /MANE-JA SAN, /MO-ICHIDO /YARINAOSI/SASETE, /KURENAIKAI?/ /380
(Oh, I've made a mistake... Hey Manager, can I do it again?")

| Hat-san said some Japanese words again and the manager said... | /390 |

【Manager】Oh, Hat-san, you said another 8 Japanese words. That's 1800 yen! /400

---- 【END】 ----

[6] 俺は熊ではない！

〔平木　茂子（Shigeko Hiraki）〕

　昨日、ＨＯＥの落語教室で「落語：シューティング・ベアズを暗記するように」との宿題が出ました。この落語の内容は次のようなものです。
　熊撃ちの大好きなブラック氏は、今日も、友人を誘ってハンティングに出掛けようとしますが、友人は嫌がります。熊と間違えて友人を撃ちかねないからです。それでもと誘うブラック氏に、友人は「俺は熊ではない」と書いた紙を背中に貼っておくから、注意しろと言います。それなのに、ブラック氏の弾は友人をかすめてしまいます。怒った友人にブラック氏は言います。おー、許してくれ、私には「ではない」の文字が見えなかったのだと……。
　この宿題を受け取って、熊さんは、どうしたでしょうか。
～～～～～～～～～～～～～～～～～～～～～～～～～～～～～～～～

【八】熊さん、どうしたんだい？　難しい顔して、紙っ切れなんか、のぞき込んじゃってさー。
【熊】八つぁん、俺、悲しいんだよー。
【八】だからさ、どうしたんだってば。アレー、これは、昨日、ＨＯＥでもらった宿題じゃないか。
【熊】ウーン……。
【八】昼休みに、コーヒーを飲みながら、宿題を暗記するのが、とっても楽しいって、熊さん、いつも、言ってたじゃないか。昨日の宿題は、楽しくないのかい。
【熊】ウーン……。
【八】何だよ、ウーン・ウーンって。宿題の「シューティング・ベアズ」が気に入らないようだけど、一体、どこが気に入らないんだよ？
【熊】ウーン……。
【八】又々、ウーンかよ……。そうか、分かった。熊撃ちの話しだから、熊さん、身につまされるんだ。
【熊】それもあるけどさ、あの話に出てくる人は、自分は熊じゃないから「俺は熊ではない！」って紙を、堂々と背中に貼れるんだよ……。でもな、八つぁん……。
【八】だから、何だって言うんだよ？

【熊】俺の場合は、「俺は熊だ！」って書かなくっちゃいけないんだよ。　　／230
それだったら、すぐに、ズドーンじゃないか。

【八】なーんだ、そんなことか。そんなら簡単だよ。お前の場合は「俺は　／240
人間の熊だ！」って書けば、いいじゃないか。

【熊】そんなこと、書いてみろよ、ミスター・ブラックのヤツ、俺を撃っ　／250
た後でこう言うさ。「おー、お許しください。アタシ、「人間の」という
字が、読めなかったんです」ってな。でも、その時は、俺は既にアノ世だ
ぜ。手遅れじゃないか。

【八】熊さん、これはな、ただの……。　　　　　　　　　　　　　　　／260

【八】いいんだよ、八つぁん、同情はいらねぇよ。俺は、いずれにしても　／270
撃たれて終わる運命〔さだめ〕なのよ。

【八】ちょっと、熊さん、どうしてそんな話しになるんだよ。　　　　　／280

【熊】八つぁんの友情、俺、信じてるぜ。そんじゃ、HOEを……。　　　／290

【八】えっ、お前の悲しみと、俺の友情と、HOEとが、どうしたって？　／300
説明してくれよ、熊さん。

【熊】親友、八つぁんでも、説明が要るか……。HOEはな……。　　　／310
H：八つぁんが、仇討ちするぜ、ブラックさんよ……
O：おめーのハートに、ズドーンと一発……
E：エンドだ、ざまみろ、おめーは地獄で、俺は天国……。
俺の、辞世の句よ……。

---- 【終り】 ----

[6] I'm Not A Bear! /100

[Shigeko Hiraki]

Yesterday, Hat-san, Kuma-san and the other students at HOE /110
received homework to memorize by the next lesson. The title is
"Shooting bears", and the content is like this; Mr.Black is
very fond of shooting bears. Today Mr.Black asks his friend to
go shooting with him. But, his friend refuses because Mr.Black
often shoots his friends by mistake. But Mr.Black asks again and
again, and at last the friend says, "OK, but I'll put a big piece
of paper that has written, 'I AM NOT A BEAR!' on my back."
Despite that warning, Mr.Black shot his friend. His friend was
so upset because Mr.Black only said, "Oh, I'm so sorry but I
couldn't see the word 'NOT'."
 After receiving this homework, what did Kuma-san do?
~~~~~~
【H】 Hey Kuma-san, you look really down. What's that paper /120
in your hand?
【K】 Oh Hat-san... I'm really sad. /130
【H】 I see. Well, I have to ask why. What's the matter? /140
Oh, that paper's homework from HOE, isn't it?
【K】 Hmm... /150
【H】 You always say that you enjoy memorizing homework with /160
a nice cup of coffee. Aren't you enjoying today's homework?
【K】 Hmm... /170
【H】 "Hmm...Hmm..." Is that all you wanna say? I guess you /180
don't like today's homework, "Shooting bears", do you?
【K】 Hmm... /190
【H】 There it is again, "Hmm..." Well, I know it's upsetting /200
for you, because the story's about shooting a bear, 'Kuma'.
(Kuma is bear in Japanese.)
【K】 True. But the main thing is that the person in that story /210
is not a bear, so he should write, "I am not a bear..."

30

【H】And?... /220

【K】But I would have to write "I am a bear", so I'd be shot /230
straight away.

【H】Oh, Kuma-san, it's simple. Just write, "I am a human bear", /240
and it'll be OK!

【K】Hat-san, if I put that message on my back, surely Mr.Black /250
will say, "Oh, I'm sorry. I couldn't read the word 'human'..."
But you know, when Mr.Black says it, I'll already be dead.

【H】Kuma-san, this isn't real... /260

【K】Hat-san, don't worry about me. Anyway, it's my destiny /270
to be shot.

【H】Why do you think so, Kuma-san? I don't get it. /280

【K】Hat-san, I know you've always been my best friend. /290
So, remember HOE...

【H】I don't understand... What does your sadness have to do /300
with my friendship and HOE?

【K】Oh, even my best friend needs it explained... OK, H.O.E; /310
"H" is for "Hat-san obviously shoots at Mr.Black!".
"O" is for "Of course the bullet will penetrate Mr.Black's heart!".
"E" is for "End of Mr.Black's life, and mine. Mr.Black's in hell,
but Kuma's in heaven!". THIS IS MY GOODBYE POEM...

---- 【END】 ----

《About Goodbye Poem》
　Goodbye Poem is
　"Jisei no ku"
　in Japanese.
　In the old days
　in Japan, people
　wrote a Goodbye
　Poem before they died.

31

[7] ワッハ上方

〔平木 茂子 (Shigeko Hiraki)〕

------------------------（飲み屋「ゆき」で）----------------------

【ゆき】いらっしゃーい。あらー、八つぁんに熊さん、来てくれて、嬉しいわ。今日は、お休みでしょ、どうしたの？

【八】ウン、千日前の「ワッハ上方」で、「英語で落語」の会があったんで、熊さんと行ってきたんだよ。ホレ、俺達、ＨＯＥインターナショナルってトコで、「英語で落語」を教わってるって、この前、話したろ。そこの主催なんだ。出演したのも、そこの生徒さん達なんだよ。

【ゆき】それで、どうだった？　面白かった？

【熊】ウン。皆、上手でさ、笑いの連続よ。終わっても、その余韻かなぁ、ゆきちゃんのトコで、楽しく、飲みたくなったんだ。

【ゆき】ありがとう。2人とも、相当に楽しんだようね。ところで、何を食べる？　いつものトリ鍋でいーい？

【八】勿論だよ。あれ、旨いもんなぁ。それと飲物は……熊さん、ビールかい、日本酒かい？

【熊】ビールがいいな。

【ゆき】分かったわ、すぐに出来るから、ビール、飲んでてね。そうなの、その「英語で落語」って、そんなに楽しかったの。私も行きたかったわ。

【八】ゆきちゃんと一緒だったら、もっと・もっと楽しかったのになぁ。

【ゆき】それで、お客さんは、入っていた？

【熊】それが、大入り満員だったんだよ。

【ゆき】まぁ、英語落語って人気があるのね。あら、鍋が煮立ってるわ。さ、トリ鍋の出来上がりよ。熱いうちに食べてね。あれ、熊さん、どうしたの、考え込んじゃって。

【八】熊さんは、今、落語を作るのに、悪戦苦闘中なんだよ。

【ゆき】落語を作るって？　熊さん、それ、ホント？

【熊】ウン。ＨＯＥの「英語で落語」の教室は、とても自由な雰囲気なんだ。それで、俺が落語を作って、八つぁんがそれを語ったら、とても良い勉強になると思って始めたんだけど、落語にはオチがつきものだろう。それが、どうしても上手く書けなくて、苦しくってさ、いつも、唸〔うな〕ってるんだよ。

【ゆき】そういえば、熊さん、少し痩せたようだわ。大変なのね。何か、／270
私に出来ることがあれば……そうだ、何か、「オチに関係ある食べ物」を
用意するわね。だって昔から言うじゃない、関係ある物を食べたりすると、
運が良くなるって。

【八】ゆきちゃん、俺にも、その「オチに関係ある食べ物」、頼むよ。／280

【ゆき】八つぁんは、いいの、熊さんだけよ。そうだ、隣の店、まだ開い／290
ているから、ちょっと、見てくるわ。勝手に食べててね……。

【八】何だよ、又、熊さんかよ。もしかしたら、ゆきちゃん……。／300

【熊】八つぁん、ゆきちゃんが帰ってきたよ。ブツブツ言うの、止めろよ。／310

【ゆき】ただいまー。あら、食べ終わったの？ じゃ、いいものを出すわ／320
ね。ホラ、これよ。おしゃれで、豪華でしょ。

【八】凄いじゃないか、これ、何て言うんだい？／330

【ゆき】フルーツ・ポンチよ。英語では、フルーツ・パンチって言うらし／340
いわ。熊さんがパンチ・ライン（オチ）に恵まれるように、パンチに関係
ある物を探したのよ。

【八】旨そうじゃないか。じゃ、いただくぜ。／350

【ゆき】八つぁん、これは、2つとも、熊さんのなの。／360

【八】えっ、俺の分は？／370

【ゆき】だって、八つぁんは、落語を書かないもの、要らないじゃない。／380

【八】そりゃ、あんまりだぜ、ゆきちゃん。さっきのトリ鍋だって、俺、／390
見ちゃったんだ。熊さんの鍋には、肉が、4つも入っていたのに、俺の
には2つだけだろ。その上、これも俺にはナシだなんて……ダブル・パンチ
で、俺、泣きたいよ、ウワーン……。

----【終り】----

[7] Rakugo Theater, "Wahha Kamigata"

[Shigeko Hiraki]

---------------------- (At the pub "Yuki") ----------------------

【Yuki】 Hi Hat-san and Kuma-san! Oh, I'm so happy you've come to my pub. You don't usually come here on your day off...

【H】 We went to Wahha Kamigata Theater at Sennichimae to hear rakugo in English. HOE International is holding rakugo Entertainment there. Like I told you before, we learn rakugo in English at HOE. Our classmates did some rakugo there.

【Yuki】 Did you enjoy it?

【K】 Yeah, a lot. All of the performers did their rakugo very well. The whole audience enjoyed it and laughed from start to finish. After that we felt refreshed, so we came here to have a nice drink with you...

【Yuki】 Thank you! I guess you have had a good time today. By the way, what would you like? If you want, I'll fix your usual food, chicken soup.

【H】 Sure. It's really tasty. We love it! Hey Kuma-san, which do you fancy, beer or sake?

【K】 I'll have a beer.

【Yuki】 OK! Your food won't be long. Have a beer first. Well... that rakugo in English sounds nice, I wish I could go there with you...

【H】 Oh, I wish Yuki-chan could have been at today's rakugo performance...

【Yuki】 How about the audience? Were there a lot of people?

【K】 It was a full house...

【Yuki】 Rakugo in English is popular now, isn't it? Hey, your special chicken soup's ready! Come and get it while it's hot. Kuma-san, what are you thinking about? You looked worried.

【H】 Kuma-san's under a lot of pressure writing rakugo.

【Yuki】 Are you really writing rakugo, Kuma-san?

【K】Yeah. The rakugo in English class has a very free /260
atomosphere. So Hat-san and I decided that I should write some
original rakugo for Hat-san to do on-stage. But the problem is
I can't find a good punch line, "ochi".

【Yuki】Kuma-san, you seem to be getting thin. I guess writing /270
rakugo is hard work for you. I'd like to help you... I know,
I'll prepare some food related to your punch line. It's said
in Japan that eating something related to what you want
brings you good luck with it.

【H】Hey, hey, Yuki-chan, prepare some of that for me, too. /280

【Yuki】Hat-san, you don't need it. Well, I'm gonna go shopping. /290
I'll be back soon. Help yourselves to some food...

【H】Yuki-chan's worried about Kuma-san again... Maybe /300
she's in love...

【K】Hey Hat-san, Yuki-chan's returned. Stop your mumbling. /310

【Yuki】Hey! I brought you a little something. Here it is. /320

【H】Oh, great! What is it? /330

【Yuki】It's fruit punch. I hope Kuma-san can find it easier /340
to write a good punch line. If he has this, I'm sure he'll
have no problem.

【H】It looks delicious. I'll have this one. /350

【Yuki】Hat-san, both are for Kuma-san. /360

【H】Where's mine? /370

【Yuki】You aren't writing rakugo, /380
so you don't need any punch.

【H】Oh, you're so mean to me. /390
As for the chicken soup, there
were four chunks of chicken on
Kuma-san's plate, but only two
on mine. And there's no punch
for me... It's a double whammy!
I'm gonna cry ... Wah...

---- 【END】 ----

[8] 我らがノラ社長

〔平木 茂子 (Shigeko Hiraki)〕

【八・熊】よーし、それじゃ、ゆきちゃんの店に行こうじゃないか……。

【ゆき】あらー、八つぁんに熊さん、今日は、金曜日じゃないのに来てくれたのね、嬉しいわ。

【八】ウン。今日は、珍しく早く終わったんでね、来ちゃったよ。

【熊】俺達、2人、この3月にこっちに来ただろ。単身赴任だから、家に帰っても、つまらなくてね、つい、ゆきちゃんの店に来ちゃうんだ。

【ゆき】そりゃ、淋しいわねぇ。美味しいもの、いっぱい作るから、出来るだけ、足をこっちに向けてちょうだいね。はい、ビールと特製サラダよ。

【八】わー旨そう！ 客がいないから、ゆきちゃんも一緒に飲もうよ。

【熊】俺達の食いもんなら後回しでいいからさ、ここに座ってくれよ。

【ゆき】そーお、それじゃ、一緒に飲むわね。コップ、持ってくる。

【八・熊・ゆき】カンパーイ！ 《ゴク・ゴク・ゴク》。あー、旨い！

【ゆき】何だか、伸び伸びとするわね。ところで今日は、落語教室に行く日じゃ、なかったの？

【熊】明日なんだ。明日の落語はもう出来上がったんだよ。後は、八つぁんが読むだけなんだ。

【ゆき】よかった。それで、今度の落語は何という題なの？

【熊】「八と熊とで二人三脚！」なんだよ。もう少し溜まったら、社長に、送るんだ。

【ゆき】えっ、どうして、落語を社長さんに？

【八】俺達2人が、こっちに来ることが決まった時、社長に言われたんだよ。「あっちに行ったら、何でもいいから、仕事以外に新しいことを始めろ。チャレンジしてみろ」って。

八と熊とで二人三脚！

【熊】ウン。俺達、そういう指導で、ここまで来られたんだよ。　　　　　/260
【ゆき】何だか、凄い社長さんなのね。　　　　　　　　　　　　　　　/270
【熊】そうなんだよ。普通の感覚じゃ理解出来ないよ。例えば、俺達は、　/280
中学を出てすぐ、この会社に入ったけど、どの会社でも相手にしてくれな
かった俺達を、「よし、ウチで頑張ってみろ」って、採ってくれたんだ。
【八】入ってからは、色々なことに、挑戦させてくれたんだよ。俺達が、　/290
出来るハズがないと思ったことでも、思い切ってやらせてくれたんだ。
【熊】俺達に、「一歩、踏み出せば出来る」ってことを教えてくれた恩人　/300
なんだよ。
【八】だから、この落語のことも、2人で、こんなに、生き生きとやって　/310
ますってこと、具体的に見せたいんだよ。落語を作って、それを喋るって、
苦しいけど、とっても楽しいんだ。その報告をしたいんだ。
【ゆき】素晴らしい社長さんなのね。お名前は、何というの？　　　　　/320
【熊】ノラ社長って言うんだ。我らがノラ社長なんだ。　　　　　　　　/330
【八】ノラ社長に、カンパーイだ。あー、酔った・酔った、いい気分だな。/340
旨い肴〔さかな〕に、旨い酒。なにより、美人のおゆきちゃん！
【ゆき】まぁ、ありがと。アタシも、久しぶりに、ホロ酔い気分だわ。　/350
【八】ゆきちゃんの酔ったの、初めてみたよ。最高だなぁ。　　　　　　/360
【ゆき】そーお、こんなことも、タマには、しなくっちゃね。　　　　　/370
【熊】そうだよ、ゆきちゃん、働くばっかりじゃ、ダメだよ。ストレスは　/380
発散しておかないと。
【八】そうだ！ 熊さん、この辺で、ストレス解消のために、川柳の作り　/390
っこをしようぜ。
【熊】そうだな、そんじゃ最初にいくぜ。「熊さんが、オチ・オチ・オチ　/400
で、四苦八苦！」とくらぁ。さぁ、次は、八っぁんだ。
【八】よーし。「八さんが、オチの所で、間違えた！」もういっちょ、い　/410
けそうだぜ。「期待した、笑い起こらず、八つ当たり！」どうだ、ピッタ
リだろ。次は、ゆきちゃんだぜ。
【ゆき】あらー、アタシに、出来るかしら。　　　　　　　　　　　　　/420
【八】何だっていいんだよ。思いついたことを言うだけなんだから。　　/430
【ゆき】そーお、それじゃ、やってみるわね。「八・熊の、努力をかって、/440
拍手して！」「……あら無いの？ も一度言うわ、♡ウッフ〜ン♡……」

---- 【終り】----

《川柳について》

　日本には、日本語の特徴を活かした短い詩がいくつかあります。川柳も、その一つです。川柳は、五・七・五の計十七の音を持ちます。前頁の川柳（日本語の落語、シーケンス"/400"の下線部分）で説明します。

------------------------------(例)------------------------------
① 熊さんが、オチ・オチ・オチで、四苦八苦　　　　　　　⇐日本語
② Ku/ma/sa/n/ga, o/chi/o/chi/o/chi/de, shi/ku/ha/k/ku　　　⇐ローマ字
③ くまさんが　おちおちおちで　しくはっく　　　　　　　⇐ひらがな
④ =====(5)=====　========(7)=========　=====(5)=====　　⇐3つの部分
⑤ Kuma-san　　　with punch-line.....　　is groaning　　　⇐英語
----

　③の行を見て下さい。ひらがなで書くと分かりやすいと思います。川柳の十七音は、五・七・五に分けて書くようになっています。川柳の規則はこれだけです。少し日本語を知っていれば、誰にでも作れるのが川柳です。この落語の八つぁん・熊さん・おゆきちゃんのように、気楽に楽しんでください。

　川柳と同じく十七音の詩で俳句というものもあります。こちらも、五・七・五に分かれていて川柳と同じですが、内容的には違います。俳句には季節を読み込まなければいけない等々、難しい規則が多いのです。落語が家庭着だとしたら、俳句は訪問着のようなものと言っていいでしょう。

[8] Our Wonderful Boss, Mr. Nora!

[Shigeko Hiraki]

【H・K】 OK! Then, let's go to Yuki-chan's pub!...

【Yuki】 Hey Hat-san and Kuma-san! I'm very happy you've come here not on a Friday.

【H】 We finished work earlier and came here on autopilot...

【K】 Yeah. We both moved to Osaka without our families this March, so, we don't wanna go home, we wanna come here!

【Yuki】 Life can be lonely... I'll fix you some good food, so please come more often. Here's your beer and salad.

【H】 Wow, it looks delicious! You don't have any customers now, so let's have a beer together.

【K】 Yeah, you don't need to fix us any food, just come and sit here.

【Yuki】 OK, I'll have a drink with you. I'll take my glass...

【H・K・Y】 Cheers! <glug, glug, glug> Really delicious!

【Yuki】 Oh, I feel so good! By the way, did you have a lesson at HOE today?

【K】 No, it's tomorrow. I'm happy today because I finished writing our rakugo and Hat-san's gonna read it on-stage tomorrow.

【Yuki】 Cool! So what's the title of this rakugo?

【K】 It's "Hat-san and Kuma-san walk with three legs!". We'll send our rakugo to our boss when we've written more.

【Yuki】 Huh? Why are you gonna send it to your boss?

【H】 When we moved to Osaka, our boss said we had to try new things beside our job.

【K】 Our boss, Nora has always been teaching us stuff like that.

【Yuki】 Wow, your boss must be a great guy...

【K】 Yeah, I don't think anybody really gets him. For example, when we took his company's recruitment exam after junior high, he just said, "OK, I'll take you on!". Not a single company gave us even a chance to take the exam. That's how it all started.

【H】After starting work there, he let us do a lot of things /290
that we never thought we could do... And we now know that we
can achieve everything we want, by just sticking with it...

【K】Mr.Nora gave us the confidence that we could do anything /300
by repeating it. He is our life-saver!

【H】So, we wanna tell him how happy we are writing rakugo /310
in Osaka and doing them on-stage. It's hard but really
interesting!

【Yuki】Wow! He sounds like a great boss! What's his name? /320

【K】His name's Mr.Nora. Our Nora! /330

【H】Three cheers for the boss, Nora! Woah, I'm drunk... /340
I feel great... Good food and good beer... And Yuki-chan
looking especially gorgeous...

【Yuki】Ooh thank you! I'm a bit tipsy, too... /350

【H】I've never seen you drunk before. It's so sweet... /360

【Yuki】Sometimes I like to do this kinda thing... /370

【K】Yeah, sometimes you just have to let your hair down. /380
Working all the time's no good for you...

【H】Hey Kuma-san, how about this idea; let's make up /390
a funny poem ("Senryu" in Japanese) and read it to let off
some steam!

【K】Yeah, great! OK, I'll go first. "Kuma-san is groaning /400
with each punch, punch line..." OK Hat-san, it's your turn.

【H】OK, here I go... "Hat-san misreads Kuma's rakugo. /410
so nobody laughs..." Oh, I can make one more. "Hat-san's
heart sinks as expected nobody laughs." Hey, it suits me
well, doesn't it? Hey, Yuki-chan, your turn.

【Yuki】Oh, can I do this? /420

【H】It's easy. Just say whatever comes into your head. /430

【Yuki】Well, I'll try... /440
"Everybody, clap Hat-san & Kuma-san for their effort,
I'm begging you..." "OK, shall we try again!?".

---- 【END】 ----

《About Senryu》

In Japan there are various short poems which are very characteristic of the Japanese language. "Senryu" is one of them. Each Senryu has 17 phonetic sounds and it's divided into three parts. The first part has five sounds, the second has seven and the third has five. See the example of Senryu below. Kuma-san tells this Senryu, at "/400", underline part, in rakugo in Japanese.

------------------------------- (Example) -------------------------------

① 熊さんが、オチ・オチ・オチで、四苦八苦　　　　　⇐Japanese
② Ku/ma/sa/n/ga, o/chi/o/chi/o/chi/de, shi/ku/ha/k/ku　⇐Roma-ji
③ くまさんが　おちおちおちで　しくはっく　　　　⇐Hiragana
④ =====(5)=====　========(7)=========　=====(5)=====　⇐3 parts
⑤ Kuma-san　　　with punch-line.....　is groaning　　⇐English

See ③-line. Furigana easily explains what a Senryu is like. Each Senryu has 17 sounds and it's divided into 3 parts. That's the only rule. If you know a little Japanese you can make it. So, enjoy Senryu-making like Hat-san, Kuma-san and Yuki-chan in this rakugo.

There is another short poem like Senryu called a "Haiku". It has 17 sounds and is divided into 3 parts just the same as a Senryu. But, it's difficult to make because seasons and so on should be included in it. We can say Senryu is like a casual clothes but Haiku is a party dress.

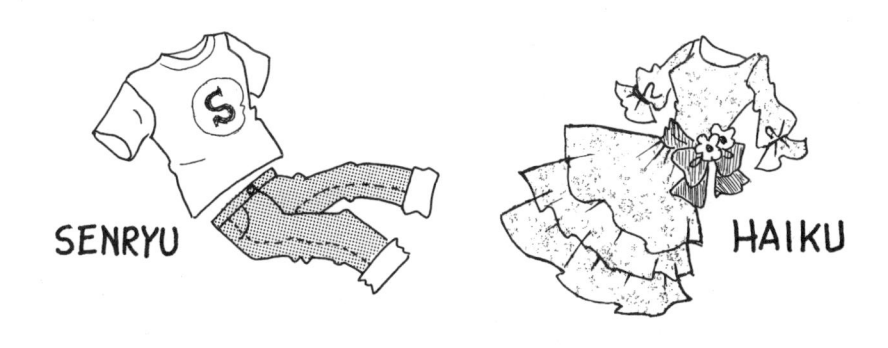

SENRYU　　　　　　HAIKU

[9] 熊さんチの猫

〔平木 茂子（Shigeko Hiraki）〕

　それでは、熊さんチの猫を紹介しよう。
　猫のファイルは、生まれてすぐに、熊さんちの軒下に捨てられていたのを助けられた。その恩義を忘れず、熊さんが、単身赴任で大阪に行ってしまった後、しっかり、家を守っている。
　ファイルは新聞を取ってくるとか、押し売りを追い払うとかは、子猫の頃からちゃんとやっていた。しかし今は、食事の際には熊さんの席に座って皆を睨んでいる。この間も食事の時にトラ助がご飯をこぼしたら、凄い唸り声で脅されたし、クルミが食事中にテレビを見たいと言ったら、チャンネルを口にくわえて放さないとか、そんなことは、日常茶飯事である。
　さて、そんな時、熊さんが、会議のために東京に帰ってきた。

〜〜〜〜〜〜〜〜〜〜〜〜〜〜〜〜〜〜〜〜〜〜〜〜〜〜〜〜〜〜〜〜〜〜〜〜〜〜〜

【熊】ただいまー。
【家族】お帰りなさーい！　お前さん！　とうちゃん！　熊！　ニャン！
【熊】おー、みんな、元気だったかい？ファイルも元気だったかい？　さぁ、ファイルこっちにお出で。ホラ、魚の旨いの買ってきたからな。俺の留守の間は、代わりをしてくれて、ありがとよ。
【千代】ちょいと、お前さん、そうやってファイルを煽〔あお〕てるものだから威張っちゃってさ……。
【熊】いいじゃないか、家を守ってくれて、可愛いじゃないか。
------------------------(さーて、その夜) ------------------------
【熊】いいか、ファイル、よく聞けよ。俺はな、今、ＨＯＥってトコで、「英語で落語」を習ってて、自分でも落語を作っているんだけど、オチが出なくて、悩んでるんだ。いいのがあったら、教えてくれよ。
【ファイル】ニャーン。
【熊】そうか。それじゃいくぜ。この話は、男、２人が、ゆきちゃんって美人を張り合う、恋愛物なんだ。

42

【ファイル】ニャン・ニャン・ニャン……。 /210
【熊】なんだよ、ファイル、どうしたってんだよ。 /220
【千代】ちょいと、お前さん、ゆきちゃんが、どうのこうのって、言っ /230
てたようだけど、ゆきちゃんって、誰だい？
【熊】あっ、ゆきちゃんっていうのが、今度の落語の、主人公なんだよ。 /240
【千代】本当かい？　何だか色っぽい名前だねぇ。 /250
【熊】えっ、そうかい、でも、落語に出てくる女は、色っぽくないと……。/260
あー危なかった。ファイル、ありがとよ。どうやら、ゆきちゃんって言葉
は、使わない方がいいな。そうだ、ちーちゃんとしよう。聞かれた時に、
「こりゃ、お前のことだよ、千代」って言えるからな。男二人も、HとK
にしとくぜ。ファイルのことだ、これが誰を意味するか、分かるだろ？
【ファイル】ニャーン。 /270
【熊】HもKも、どっちも、ちーちゃんが、自分に惚れてるって思ってい /280
るようだが、実際は、ちーちゃんは、Kの方に、気があるんだ。
【ファイル】ニャン？ /290
【熊】何だよ、ファイル、その疑わしい声と、その目つき。ホントだぜ。 /300
何故かというと、ちーちゃんの店で、例えば、鳥鍋を注文すると、俺……
オットット違った、そのKの方には、肉が倍は入っているんだ。ま、そん
なこんなで、結局、Hの方が、自分から身をひくんだ。この辺りが、この
恋愛物の、山場なんだ。
【ファイル】ニャン！ /310
【熊】そうか、面白いか。だけどな、これで終わりじゃないんだ。問題が /320
あるんだ。俺って、家族を大切にするタイプだろう。だから、二人の子供
を残して、ちーちゃんのトコには行けないし、それに、大切なおっかぁを
一人にしておけないし、ファイルとも分かれたくないし……何より、俺、
千代のこと、大好きなんだ。全部、連れて、ちーちゃんの所に行くっての
もなぁ……。あー、千代、千代、どうしよう……。
【千代】ちょいと、お前さん、目をお覚ましよ。フトンの上で、暴れちゃ /330
ってさ。千代、千代って、私はここだよ。まぁ、お前さんって、そんなに
アタシのことを……。
【熊】えっ、今のは夢？　あー、よかった。もうちょっとで俺、大阪に、 /340
大きな家を、借りるトコだったよ……。

---- 【終り】 ----

[9] Kuma-san's Cat

[Shigeko Hiraki]

    Now let's introduce Kuma-san's cat.
    His name is File. He was dumped on Kuma-san's doorstep as soon as he'd been born. Kuma-san's family saved File's life and he'll never forget that. When Kuma-san moved to Osaka alone, File looked after Kuma-san's family for him.
    All his life, File fetched newspapers, chased off bad salesmen and so on. But now, at mealtimes, he sits on Kuma-san's seat and watches the family. When Torasuke spilt some rice on the table a few days ago, File stared and growled at him, and when Kurumi wants to watch TV at mealtimes, File holds the TV remote control in his mouth. He always does things like that.
    One day, Kuma-san returned to Tokyo for a meeting.

～～～～～～～～～～～～～～～～～～～～～～～～～～～～～～

【K】Hi! I'm home...
【All-family】Hi darling! Hi daddy! Hey Kuma! Miaow!
【K】So is everybody well? How about you, File? Come on, here's a nice fish for you. Thanks for looking after my house for me.
【C】You always flatter File like this, he's getting a big head...
【K】It's OK, Chiyo. He's protecting my family... He's great...
------------------------ (That night) --------------------------
【K】Hey File, listen to me carefully. I'm crazy about rakugo in English now and I'm writing some rakugo myself. But the problem is that I can't write a punch line... Please help me if you have a good idea.
【F】Miaow...
【K】OK! This story is about love; two men love the same beautiful lady called Yuki-chan.

【F】 Miaow, miaow, miaow... /210
【K】 Hey File, what's the matter with you? /220
【C】 Kuma, you said something about Yuki-chan. Who's Yuki-chan? /230
【K】 Oh, um, Yuki-chan is the heroine of my rakugo... /240
【C】 Really?... That name sounds attractive... /250
【K】 Um... But a rakugo heroine needs to be attractive... Phew, /260
I got away with it! Thank you, File! I shouldn't say Yuki-chan,
I'll say Chi-chan. When she asks me, I can answer "Chi-chan means
you, Chiyo, of course!". And, I'll say H and K for the two men.
File, you can easily guess who H and K are, can't you?
【F】 Miaow! /270
【K】 Hey File, H and K both think Chi-chan loves him but /280
as a matter of fact, Chi-chan loves only K.
【F】 Miaow? /290
【K】 Oh File, you look and sound doubtful... I'm telling /300
the truth. Because, for example, H and K ordered chicken soup
at Chi-chan's snack bar and my... oh no, not mine, but K's plate
was full of chicken, maybe a double portion of it. And so on
and so on. Finally, H went away from Chi-chan.
It's the climax of this love story.
【F】 Miaow! /310
【K】 Oh interesting? But, that's not all. I have a big problem. /320
I love my family very much. So I'll never go to Chi-chan's
house and leave my kids... I'll never leave my mum and I always
want to be with File... And... I love Chiyo, my wife. I feel
like I have to go to Chi-chan's house and take all of my family
with me... Oh, what shall I do? Chiyo, Chiyo...
【C】 Hey Kuma, wake up! Why are you tossing and turning on /330
the bed? You were saying, "Chiyo, Chiyo..." I'm right here
with you. Oh, you love me so much...
【K】 What? It's a dream? Oh, what a relief... /340
I'm gonna rent a big house in Osaka for everyone...

---- 【END】 ----

[10] ワンダフルジャパン　　　　　　　　　　　　　　　/100

〔山本　正昭（Yamamoto Masaaki）1990〕

~~~~~~
　アメリカのとある片田舎に大きな若者がいた。彼の名はジェフ・スミス。/110
その小さな町にはたった一つの映画館と学校、そして消防署もたった一つ。
彼はそんな小さな町から一度も出たことがなかった。ところが山本ケンと
いう日本の青年が、彼の町を訪ね二人は大の仲良しとなり、今度はジェフ
に日本に来ないかと誘った。こうしてこの若きアメリカ青年ジェフは日本
に行くことになった。
~~~~~~
【フライトアテンダント】当機はまもなく関西国際空港へと到着致します。/120
皆様、お席にお戻りになり、シートベルトをお締め下さいますようお願い
申し上げます。
【ジェフ】わぁ、いよいよ日本に着くのだな。ほんと、家と車がいっぱい！/130
人もたくさん歩いている！　いよいよ着陸だな。あっ着いた。全然揺れな
いよ、素晴らしい着陸だ！　きっとパイロットはいい腕しているんだな。
素晴らしい！
【フライトアテンダント】当機は只今関西国際空港に着陸致しました。本　/140
日も当機をご利用頂きまして誠にありがとうございました。またのご搭乗
を心よりお待ち致しております。さよなら。
【ジェフ】わぁ、きれいな声のお姉さんだな。　　　　　　　　　　/150
【フライトアテンダント】お気をつけて、良い旅をなさって下さい。　　/160
さよなら。
【ジェフ】ありがとう、さよなら。ここが入国審査だな、すごーい人。ど　/170
こに並べばいいのかな？　ここはちがうな「日本在住者」って書いている
ものね。ここは「エイリアン」！？　エイリアン？　僕は他の星から来た
わけじゃないのに。でもおかしいな、他に並ぶところもないから、きっと
ここだな。
【入国審査官】パスポート！　　　　　　　　　　　　　　　　　　/180
【ジェフ】ハイ、どうぞ。　　　　　　　　　　　　　　　　　　　/190
【入国審査官】お仕事で来られたのですか？それとも観光ですか？　　/200
【ジェフ】観光です。　　　　　　　　　　　　　　　　　　　　　/210

【入国審査官】そうですか。どれくらい日本に滞在する予定ですか？　　　　/220
【ジェフ】だいたい2週間くらいです。　　　　　　　　　　　　　　　/230
【入国審査官】わかりました。（スタンプを押す）これで結構です。　　　/240
【ジェフ】ありがとう、さよなら。あぁ怖かった。ケンが空港まで来てく　/250
れていたらいいんだけどな。ケンは何処かな？　ケンは何処かな？　あぁ
いた！　いた！　ケン！　ここだよ。僕だよ、ジェフだよ。ケン！
【ケン】ジェフ！　こっち、こっち。ジェフ、調子はどう？　　　　　　/260
【ジェフ】最高！　　　　　　　　　　　　　　　　　　　　　　　　/270
【ケン】日本にようこそ！　　　　　　　　　　　　　　　　　　　　/280
【ジェフ】空港まで迎えに来てくれてありがとう。　　　　　　　　　　/290
【ケン】とんでもないよ。それよりジェフ、空の旅はどうだった？　　　/300
【ジェフ】最高！　それに飛行機も揺れなかったしね。　　　　　　　　/310
【ケン】それは良かったね。じゃー時差ボケもナシ？　　　　　　　　　/320
【ジェフ】ない、ない。時差ボケなんて無縁さ！　飛行機は本当に快適だ　/330
ったよ。スチュワーデスのお姉さんは綺麗で優しいし、日本の女の人大好
き！　日本は素晴らしいよ、僕日本が大好きになっちゃった。
【ケン】良かった、良かった。さあ行こうか。　　　　　　　　　　　　/340
【ジェフ】オッケー。わあ、人がたくさんいる！　ケン、今日はお祭りか　/350
何かあるの？
【ケン】お祭りなんてないさ。いつもこんな感じだよ。　　　　　　　　/360
【ジェフ】いつもこんな感じ？　ふ～ん。あっケン！　ケン！　　　　　/370
【ケン】どうしたの。　　　　　　　　　　　　　　　　　　　　　　/380
【ジェフ】日本人は何処にいるの？　　　　　　　　　　　　　　　　/390
【ケン】えっ、今何て言った？　　　　　　　　　　　　　　　　　　/400
【ジェフ】誰が日本人なの？　　　　　　　　　　　　　　　　　　　/410
【ケン】誰って、皆日本人さ。　　　　　　　　　　　　　　　　　　/420
【ジェフ】ええ？でも誰も着物着ていないよ。　　　　　　　　　　　/430
【ケン】ああそういう事か。最近は誰も着物なんてきないよ。でも皆日本　/440
人なんだよ。分かった？　じゃあ、タクシーに乗ろうよ。
【ジェフ】オーケー。わあ！　ケン！　君は魔法使いかい？　　　　　　/450
【ケン】何だって？　　　　　　　　　　　　　　　　　　　　　　　/460
【ジェフ】君は魔法使いかと聞いたんだ。　　　　　　　　　　　　　/470
【ケン】そんな訳ないだろ。どうかしたの？　　　　　　　　　　　　/480
【ジェフ】だってケンは何にもさわってないのに、ドアが開いたんだよ。　/490

【ケン】ハハハ。日本ではタクシーのドアは皆自動で開くんだ。

【ジェフ】そうだったのか。すごい！ ドアが自動で開くなんていいサービスだよね。日本は素晴らしい国だよ。僕、ますます日本が気に入ったな。

【ケン】さあ乗って。

【ジェフ】うん。

【タクシーの運転手】どちらまで、行きましょうか？

【ケン】梅田までお願いします。

【ジェフ】ケン、これ何？ 運転手さんが僕にティシュくれたよ。

【ケン】ああこれ？ 運転手さんがジェフにあげるって。

【ジェフ】ティシュただでくれるの？ すご〜いサービス！ ねえケン。「サンキュー」って日本語でどう言うの？

【ケン】「ありがとう」って言うんだよ。

【ジェフ】あり、あり、、、難しい！ 僕言えないよ。

【ケン】簡単だよ。「アリゲーター（ワニ）」って言えばいいんだ。クロコダイル（ワニ）のことだよ。知ってるだろ。

【ジェフ】うん、知っているよ。

【ケン】アリゲーターって言ってみて。

【ジェフ】そうなんだ。アリゲーター！

【タクシーの運転手】どう致しまして。

【ジェフ】ケン、あの人今何て言ったの？

【ケン】「どう致しまして」これは「ユア、ウエルカム」の意味なんだ。だ。

【ジェフ】ふ〜ん。ど、ど、どう、、、ああこれも難しい！

【ケン】大丈夫、このフレーズを覚えておけばいいよ。「ドン、タッチ、マイ、マスタッシュ」

【ジェフ】ドン、タッチ、マイ、マスタッシュ？

【ケン】その通り。それを速く言えばいいんだ。ドンタッチマイマスタッシュ、ドンタッチマイマスタッシュ、ドウイタシマシテ。

【ジェフ】オーケー。ドンタッチマイマスタッシュ、ドンタッチマイマスタッシュ。

【ケン】もういいよ。もう充分だよ。

【ジェフ】わあ！ 見て、見て！ テレビじゃないか。このタクシー、テレビ付きなんだね。あっ電話もあるじゃん。日本のサービスって、ほんとすごい！

【ケン】ジェフ、もう着いたよ。さあ降りて。	/750
【ジェフ】うん。わあ！ 日本ってほんとに近代的だね。ヒルトンホテル！あそこにヒルトンホテルだ。	/760
【ケン】ねえジェフ。悪いんだけど僕、大事な仕事が残ってて、行かなくてはいけないんだ。だから2時間ほどその辺散歩でもして、時間潰してもらえないかな。	/770
【ジェフ】大丈夫だよ。それも楽しいかも。じゃあ、どこで会おうか？	/780
【ケン】そうだな、6時にマルビルの前はどう？見て！ここがマルビルだよ。いい？	/790
【ジェフ】うん。ここがマルビルだね。じゃあ6時にね。	/800
【ケン】ジェフ、散歩楽しんでね。バイバイ。	/810
【ジェフ】ケン、ありがとう。クロコダイル！（種類の違うワニ）	/820
【ケン】違うよ、アリゲーター！	/830
【ジェフ】ごめん、ごめん。アリゲーター！ バイバイ。ケンっていい奴だよな。それにしてもいい天気だな。あっありがとう。ティッシュくれるの？ アリゲーター。えっ、またくれるの？ アリゲーター。日本って本当にお金持ちなんだな。。。あそこに若くて美しい、日本の女の人がいるけど、声かけたいな。でも彼女こっちの方に近寄って来る、どうしょう。	/840
【日本女性】あのう、すみません。お話してもいいですか？	/850
【ジェフ】もちろん！	/860
【日本女性】ありがとう。日本は好きですか。	/870
【ジェフ】ええ。大好きだよ。	/880
【日本女性】どこから来たの。	/890
【ジェフ】アメリカのテキサス。	/900
【日本女性】いくつなの。	/910
【ジェフ】１９歳です。	/920
【日本女性】まあ１９歳なの。ありがとう、バイバイ。	/930
【ジェフ】バ〜イ。あんな綺麗な人が声をかけて来るなんて、わくわくするな。日本、大〜好き。	/940
【日本人その2】失礼ですが、お話させて頂いてよろしいですか？	/950
【ジェフ】もちろんいいですよ。	/960
【日本人その2】日本はお好きですか。	/970
【ジェフ】ええ、大好きです。	/980

【日本人その２】どこから来られたのですか。　　　　　　　　　　/990
【ジェフ】テキサスから来ました。　　　　　　　　　　　　　　　/1000
【日本人その２】おいくつですか。　　　　　　　　　　　　　　　/1010
【ジェフ】１９歳です。　　　　　　　　　　　　　　　　　　　　/1020
【日本人その２】そうなんですか、ありがとう。さようなら。　　　/1030
【ジェフ】さよなら。日本の人ってホント、フレンドリーだな。日本、大　/1040
〜好き。
【日本人その３】すみません、お話してもいいですか？　　　　　　/1050
【ジェフ】もちろんいいですよ。　　　　　　　　　　　　　　　　/1060
【日本人その３】日本は好きですか。　　　　　　　　　　　　　　/1070
【ジェフ】ええ、大好きです。　　　　　　　　　　　　　　　　　/1080
【日本人その３】どこから来たのですか。　　　　　　　　　　　　/1090
【ジェフ】テキサスから来ました。　　　　　　　　　　　　　　　/1100
【日本人その３】年はいくつですか。　　　　　　　　　　　　　　/1110
【ジェフ】１９歳です。　　　　　　　　　　　　　　　　　　　　/1120
【日本人その３】ああそうですか、ありがとう。さようなら。　　　/1130
【ジェフ】さよなら。ふう、今日はインタビューが多いな。ルイ・ヴィト　/1140
ンのハンドバッグだ！　高いのにな。あっ、あの女の子も持ってる。あの
子もだ。皆持っているじゃないか。日本人は皆お金持ちだな。
【日本人その４】すみません。写真撮ってもいいですか。　　　　　/1150
【ジェフ】いいですよ。カメラ貸して。　　　　　　　　　　　　　/1160
【日本人その４】違うんです。あなたと一緒に撮りたいんです。　　/1170
【ジェフ】えっ、僕と？もちろんオーケーだよ。あっ君の友達も一緒だね。/1180
「チーズ」「ちース！」
【日本人その４】ありがとう。ホントにありがとうね！　バイバイ。　/1190
【ジェフ】バ〜イ。僕何だか映画スターになったみたい。日本って素晴ら　/1200
しい！ああ、もうすぐ６時だよ。遅れるよ！
【日本人その５】すみませ〜ん、すみませ〜ん。お話してもいいですか。/1210
【ジェフ】はい。　　　　　　　　　　　　　　　　　　　　　　　/1220
【日本人その５】日本は好きですか。　　　　　　　　　　　　　　/1230
【ジェフ】はい、とっても。　　　　　　　　　　　　　　　　　　/1240
【日本人その５】どこから来られたのですか。　　　　　　　　　　/1250
【ジェフ】テキサスから来て、１９歳だよ。バイバイ。もう６時だ。遅れ　/1260
る！　マルビルはどこにあるの。ケンはどこにいるんだ。ケン！　ケン！

【ケン】ジェフ、ジェフ！　　　　　　　　　　　　　　　　　　　　　　　/1270
【ジェフ】ケン！　僕もちょうど探していたところなんだよ、よかった。　　/1280
【ケン】それはちょうどよかった。楽しく過ごせたかい？　　　　　　　　　/1290
【ジェフ】もちろんだよ。　　　　　　　　　　　　　　　　　　　　　　　/1300
【ケン】よかった。日本は好き？　　　　　　　　　　　　　　　　　　　　/1310
【ジェフ】日本は好きかって？　日本は好きって聞いてるの？　もちろん　　/1320
好きだよ。それで僕はテキサスから来て、１９歳なんだ！

【ＨＯＥでは毎年ＨＯＥ寄席（英語落語会）を催しています。】

[10] Wonderful Japan   /100

[Masaaki Yamamoto (1990)]

~~~~~~

There's a young man, a big young man. He lives in a small /110
country town in America. His name is Jeff Smith. In this town,
there's only one movie theater, only one school and only one fire
station. So, it's a very, very small town. He has never, he has
never experienced going outside of his hometown. But last year a
Japanese man, Ken Yamamoto visited his town, and they became good,
good friends. So, the Japanese man, Ken invited him to come to
Japan, and the young American, Jeff decided to go to Japan.
~~~~~~

【Flight Attendant】May I have your attention, please. We'll be /120
landing at Kansai International airport soon, so please return to
your seat and fasten your seatbelt.

【Jeff】Wow! I will be landing in Japan soon. Wow! There are /130
many houses and cars. So many people are walking! Oh, now I'm
landing. Good landing. It's very smooth. The pilot is very
good! Excellent!

【Flight Attendant】We are now arriving at Kansai International /140
airport. Thank you very much for flying with us. We hope to see
you again. Sayonara!

【Jeff】Wow! She has a beautiful voice. /150

【Flight Attendant】Have a nice trip. Sayonara. /160

【Jeff】Oh, thank you. Bye, bye. Wow, here's the immigration. /170
It's so crowded. Where should I line up? This is the Japanese
residence. Oh, that's not it. This is the alien. Alien? I'm
not from another planet. Oh, it's strange. There are no other
places. It must be here.

【Immigration】Passport, please. /180

【Jeff】Here you are. /190

【Immigration】Are you here on business or for sightseeing? /200

【Jeff】Sightseeing. /210
【Immigration】OK. How long are you planning to stay? /220
【Jeff】About two weeks. /230
【Immigration】OK. (Stamp a passport.) Thank you. /240
【Jeff】Thank you. Bye, bye. Oh, it's scary. I hope Ken meets me /250
at the airport. Oh, where's Ken? Where's Ken? Oh, there's Ken!
Hey Ken! Here I am. It's me, Jeff. Hey Ken!
【Ken】Oh, Jeff. Come over here, come over here. Oh, Jeff. How /260
are you?
【Jeff】Fine. /270
【Ken】Welcome to Japan. /280
【Jeff】Thank you for coming to the airport. /290
【Ken】You are welcome. How was your flight, Jeff? /300
【Jeff】It was great! There was no turbulence. /310
【Ken】That's good. Do you have jet lag? /320
【Jeff】No, no, no. No jet lag. I feel fine. It was a very /330
comfortable flight, because the flight attendants are so kind and
nice. I love Japanese ladies. Japan is a wonderful country. I
like Japan.
【Ken】Oh, that's good. OK. Let's go. /340
【Jeff】OK. Wow! There are so many people. Ken, is today a /350
festival?
【Ken】Oh, no, no, no. Always like this. /360

At the airport

【Jeff】Always like this? I see. Ken! /370
【Ken】Yes. /380
【Jeff】Where are the Japanese? /390
【Ken】What did you say? /400
【Jeff】Who are the Japanese? /410
【Ken】They are all Japanese. /420
【Jeff】But nobody wears a Kimono. /430
【Ken】I know what you mean. Now-a-days nobody wears the kimono. /440
But they are all Japanese, OK? Let's get a taxi.
【Jeff】OK. Wow! Wow! Ken! Are you a magician? /450
【Ken】What? /460

53

【Jeff】Are you a magician? /470

【Ken 】No, no, no.　Why? /480

【Jeff】Because, the taxi door opened, but you didn't touch it. /490

【Ken 】No, no, no.　In Japan, every taxi has an automatic door. /500

【Jeff】That's great.　Doors open automatically!　It's a good /510
service.　Japan is a wonderful country.　I like Japan.

【Ken 】OK.　Please get in. /520

【Jeff】OK. /530

【Taxi Driver 】Dochila made mairimashoka? /540

【Ken 】Umeda made onegaishimasu. /550

【Jeff】Ken, what's this?　He gave me a tissue paper.　Kleenex. /560

【Ken 】Yes, it's a gift for you. /570

【Jeff】It's a good service.　Free tissue.　OK.　Ken, how do you /580
say, "thank you" in Japanese?

【Ken 】We say, "Aligato". /590

【Jeff】Ali …?　Oh, I can't say it. /600

【Ken 】OK.　OK.　Then, remember this, "Alligator".　You know the /610
crocodile.

【Jeff】Yes, yes. /620

【Ken 】Just say, "Alligator". /630

【Jeff】Oh, that's easy.　Alligator! /640

【Taxi Driver 】Doitashimashite. /650

【Jeff】Ken, what did he say? /660

【Ken 】He said, "Doitashimashite".　It means, "You're welcome". /670

【Jeff】I see.　Doi …?　I can't say it. /680

【Ken 】OK.　Remember this phrase, "Don't touch my moustache". /690

【Jeff】Don't touch my moustache? /700

【Ken 】If you say it much faster, like this, "Don't touch my mous /710
tache".

【Jeff】OK.　Don't touch my moustache.　Don't touch my moustache… /720

【Ken 】OK. That's enough. /730

【Jeff】Wow!　Look!　It's a television isn't it?　This taxi has a /740
television.　Oh, telephone, too.　Japan has good services.

【Ken 】OK.　Here we are.　Jeff, please get out. /750

【Jeff】OK. Wow! Japan is very modern. Oh, Hilton Hotel, Hilton /760
Hotel is over there.

【Ken 】Oh, Jeff. I'm sorry. I have some important business. I /770
must go. OK? It's now four o'clock. I'll be back here at six
o'clock. So, could you please kill time looking around the city
for two hours?

【Jeff】No problem. That sounds great. Where shall we meet? /780

【Ken 】We'll meet here in front of the Maru Building at six /790
o'clock. Look! This is the Maru Building. OK?

【Jeff】OK. This is the Maru building. At six o'clock? /800

【Ken 】Right. Jeff, please enjoy taking a walk. Bye, bye. /810

【Jeff】Ken, thank you. Crocodile! /820

【Ken 】No. Alligator! /830

【Jeff】Sorry, alligator! Bye, bye. He is a nice man. Wow! It's /840
a beautiful day. Hi. Oh, thank you. Free tissue!? Alligator!
Oh, more tissue. Alligator! Japan is rich country. They gave
me free tissue. There's a beautiful young Japanese lady. I wish
I could talk to her. She is coming this way.

【Japanese Lady 】Excuse me. May I speak to you? /850

【Jeff】Oh, yes! Yes! /860

【Japanese Lady 】Thank you. Do you like Japan? /870

【Jeff】Yes, I do very much. /880

【Japanese Lady 】Where are you from? /890

【Jeff】I'm from Texas. /900

【Japanese Lady 】How old are you? /910

【Jeff】I'm nineteen years old. /920

【Japanese Lady 】Nineteen. Thank you. Bye, bye! /930

【Jeff】Bye. The beautiful lady spoke to me. That was exciting. /940
I like Japan.

【Japanese #2 】Excuse me. May I speak to you? /950

【Jeff】Oh, yes, yes. /960

【Japanese #2 】Do you like Japan? /970

【Jeff】Oh, yes, I do very much. /980

【Japanese #2 】Where are you from? /990

【Jeff】I'm from Texas. /1000
【Japanese #2】How old are you? /1010
【Jeff】I'm nineteen years old. /1020
【Japanese #2】OK. Thank you. Bye, bye. /1030
【Jeff】Bye, bye. Japanese people are so friendly. I like Japan. /1040
【Japanese #3】Excuse me. May I speak to you? /1050
【Jeff】Again? OK, yes. /1060
【Japanese #3】OK. Do you like Japan? /1070
【Jeff】Yes, I do very much. /1080
【Japanese #3】Where are you from? /1090
【Jeff】I'm from Texas. /1100
【Japanese #3】How old are you? /1110
【Jeff】I'm nineteen years old. /1120
【Japanese #3】OK. I see. Thank you. Bye, bye. /1130
【Jeff】Bye. So many interviews. A Ruibiton hand bag. Oh, maybe /1140 she is rich. Very expensive bag. Oh, look! That girl has, too. And she does, too. And everybody has a Ruibiton hand bag. Japan is a rich country.
【Japanese #4】Excuse me. May I take a picture? /1150
【Jeff】OK, give me your camera. /1160
【Japanese #4】No, no, no. I want to take a picture with you. /1170
【Jeff】With me? Sure! OK, C'mon. Oh, your friend. Say /1180 "Cheese"? OK, cheese!
【Japanese #4】Thank you. Thank you very much. Bye, bye! /1190
【Jeff】Bye. I'm like a movie star. Wow! Japan is a wonderful /1200 country. Oh, no. It's almost six o'clock. I'll be late.
【Japanese #5】Excuse me. Excuse me. May I speak to you? /1210
【Jeff】Yes. /1220
【Japanese #5】Do you like Japan? /1230
【Jeff】Yes, I do very much. /1240
【Japanese #5】Where are from? /1250
【Jeff】I'm from Texas, and I'm nineteen years old. Bye, bye. /1260 Oh, it's six o'clock. I'm late. Where is the Maru Building? Where is Ken? Where's Ken?

【Ken 】Hey.　Hey.　Jeff!　　　　　　　　　　　　　　　　　　　　　/1270
【Jeff】Oh, Ken.　Good.　I was just looking for you.　　　　　　　/1280
【Ken 】Oh, that's good.　Did you have a good time?　　　　　　　/1290
【Jeff】Yeah!　　　　　　　　　　　　　　　　　　　　　　　　　/1300
【Ken 】Good!　Do you like Japan?　　　　　　　　　　　　　　　　/1310
【Jeff】Do I like Japan? Do I like Japan?　Yes, I do very much!　/1320
I'm from Texas, and I'm nineteen years old!

Ⅲ.《落語集》八つぁん・熊さんと水泳の流体力学　　　　　　　　　/010

　　　　[11]　新・ガールフレンド　　　　　　　　　　　　　　/100

　　　　　　　　　　　〔平木 茂子（Shigeko Hiraki）〕

------------------------（プールサイドで）------------------------　/110
【熊】今日はプールが混んでるなぁ、どのコースで泳ごうか？　八つぁん、/120
八つぁんてば。何、探しているんだよ。
【八】俺のお目当ては……カオリちゃん、ショッキング・ピンクの水着の　/130
カオリちゃん……。あっ、いたいた、2コースで泳いでるな。なんだよ、
なんで野郎どもがあのコースに溢れているんだよ。これじゃ俺が、2コー
スに入れないじゃないか。
【熊】八つぁん、何をカッカしてるんだい。誰が、どのコースで泳ごうと　/140
勝手だろ。そうか、お前、水の中からカオリちゃんを観察したいんだな。
【八】ち、違うってば、熊さん、何で俺が、そんなこと……。　　　　　/150
【熊】おいおい、八つぁん、4コースで、いつものドデカ・バーサンが泳　/160
いでいるぞ。あの人、どう見ても、70歳に近いと思うが、泳ぎは上手い
なぁ。並んで泳ぐと、スイスイ、抜かれちゃうんだ。
【八】そうなんだ。河馬みたいにでっかいのに、イルカみたいに軽やかに　/170
泳ぐんだから……。

【熊】八つぁん、あれだけ上手に泳げるってことは、昔、水泳の選手だっ　　/180
たんじゃないのかなぁ。
【八】そうだろうよ。だから、上手なんだ。　　　　　　　　　　　　　　/190
【熊】八つぁん、一度、彼女と、コーヒーでも飲みながら話をしてみない　　/200
か。どうしてあんな泳ぎが出来るのか、聞いてみたいんだよ。
【八】そりゃいい考えだな。それじゃ、熊さん、ちょっと、声、かけてみ　　/210
て……。
【熊】八つぁんよ、いくらウバ桜だって、相手は女だぜ。ナンパの担当は　　/220
八つぁんって、決まってるよ。
【八】こういうことになると、熊さん、いつも俺に押しつけるんだから。　　/230
仕方がない、「相手にとって不足あり」だけど、声、掛けてみるか。もし
もし、素敵なアナタ、水泳がお上手ですねぇ！
【ドデカ・バーサン】あら、私、そんなこと言われて、嬉しいわ。練習が　　/240
終わったら、前の飲み屋でデートしません。ビールでも奢らせてもらうわ。
【八】ちょっと、ちょっと、熊さん、俺よりウワテのバーサンだぜ。こり　　/250
ゃ、熊さんに、バトンタッチだ。
【熊】えっ、八つぁんがダメなものを、どうして俺に出来るんだよ。とに　　/260
かく、やってみるけどさ……。えーと、ビールを奢ってくれるって、本当
ですか？　嬉しいなぁ。それじゃ、8時に、前の飲み屋ってことでは？
【ドデカ・バーサン】そうしましょ。今夜は楽しくなりそうね。それじゃ　　/270
ビールは私持ち、それ以外は、色男のお二人さん持ち、ってことでね。
【八・熊】えっ？　　　　　　　　　　　　　　　　　　　　　　　　　　/280
～～～～～～～～～～～～～～～～～～～～～～～～～～～～～～～～～
【八】へぇー、この飲み屋、初めて入ったけど、感じのいい店だなぁ……　　/290
初めまして。俺、八太郎、八つぁんでーす！
【熊】俺、熊助です。熊さんって、呼ばれていまーす。　　　　　　　　　/300
【ドデカ・バーサン】左が八つぁんで、右が熊さんなのね。私、マリです。　/310
マリちゃんって、呼んでね。ちょいとー、お兄さん、生ビールの大、3つ、
持って来てー！
【従業員】ハーイ、生ビール、大、3つですね。すぐ、お持ちします。　　/320
【八】あー、喉がカラッカラだよ。　　　　　　　　　　　　　　　　　　/330
【マリ】じゃ、二人は向こう側に座ってね。私は大きいからこっちに座る　　/340
わ。私の若い頃は、背の高い女はジロジロ見られたものよ。
【熊】そうか……。　　　　　　　　　　　　　　　　　　　　　　　　　/350

【マリ】でも、私、主人と知り合えたのよ。主人は私より背が低くてね、 /360
でも、「俺は背の高い女が好きだ」って言ってくれたのよ。主人が亡く
なって、もう5年になるわ。
【八・熊】そうだったのか。でも、幸せだったんだ……。 /370
【マリ】私の若い頃の夢は、ハイヒールを履いて町を歩くことだったけど、 /380
それは諦めていたの。でも、私の誕生日に、主人が赤いハイヒールを贈っ
くれてね、私は、嬉しくて嬉しくて、夜は枕元に飾って寝たのよ。
【熊】良いご主人だったんだ。 /390
【マリ】あら、私、どうして主人のことなんか話したのかしら。主人は、 /400
熊さんに似てたの。だから思い出したんだわ。
【従業員】ハーイ、生ビール、お持ちしました。他に、ご注文は？ /410
【マリ】そうねぇ、泳いだ後で、お腹がペコペコだから、いっぱい食べた /420
いわ。八つぁんと熊さんは、何がいい？
【八】ドデカ……じゃない、マリちゃん、何か選んでくれるかい。 /430
【マリ】そーお、それじゃ、お兄さん、じゃがバターと、焼き鳥と、ニシ /440
ンの塩焼きと、焼きナスと、漬物と、お握りと、そうそう、今は、ギンナ
ンの季節だからそれと……とりあえず、それ、ぜーんぶ持って来て。
【熊】そんなに、食べ切れないんじゃ……。 /450
【マリ】大丈夫よ。余ったら持って帰って、明日の朝、食べるから。 /460
【八】さすが、ドデカバ……。 /470
【マリ】ねぇねぇ、ドデカバって、私のこと？　さっきから、何度も言っ /480
たでしょ。私は、こんなに大きいから、子供の頃から、トン子とか、カバ
ちゃんとか言われ続けてきたもんだから、気になって……。

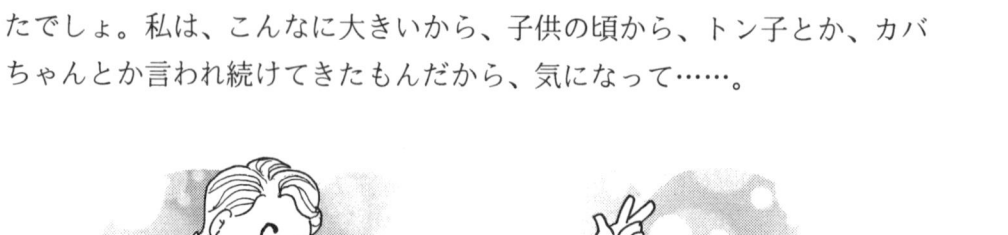

【八】えっ、そ、そんなこと、言うハズないだろ。これは俺達二人の暗号　/490
なんだ。「ハッピー！」って意味なんだよ。
【マリ】まぁ、「ハッピー！」って、ドデカバって言うの？！　暗号って　/500
面白いのねぇ。メモしといて、私も使うわ。
【八・熊】えっ……。　/510
【マリ】八つぁん、熊さん、じゃ、カンパイしましょう。私達のドデカバ　/520
な出会いを祝して、カンパーイ！
【八・熊】そ、そうだ！　ド、ドデカバー！　/530
【八・熊・マリ】《ゴクゴクゴク》あー、旨い！　/540
【従業員】お待たせー。お料理、ここに置きまーす。　/550
【マリ】さぁさぁ、熱いうちに食べましょう。ここは味が良いのよ。これ　/560
で、値段が安いとねぇ。
【八・熊】えっ、高いのかい？　/570
【マリ】冗談、冗談よ。ここは、すっごく安いのよ。さ、八つぁんに熊さ　/580
ん、ジャンジャン、食べてね。
【八】ジャンジャン食えって言われても……お、俺達持ちじゃないか……。　/590
【マリ】えっ、何か、言った？　/600
【八】いやいや何も。それじゃ俺、焼き鳥を……何だこりゃ、串だけ？　/610
【マリ】あら、八つぁん、ごめん。焼き鳥は、私が全部、食べちゃったの。　/620
八つぁんは、焼きナスでも食べてね。ここのは、美味しいから。
【八】えっ、全部、食べちゃった？　/630
【熊】八つぁん、焼きナスも美味しそうじゃないか。じゃ俺、ギンナンが　/640
好きだから、それ、もらうぜ。アレレ、カラばっかり……。
【マリ】熊さん、ごめんごめん。それも、私が……。　/650
【熊】いいんだよ、マリちゃん。俺は、漬物があれば、それで充分なんだ。　/660
ところで、マリちゃんの家は、この近くなのかい。
【マリ】そうなの。つい最近、近くに引っ越してきたの。主人に先立たれ　/670
てからは一人暮らしをしてたけど、娘が、一緒に住もうって言ったもんで。
【熊】親孝行な娘さんなんだ！　/680
【マリ】とんでもない、大違いよ。娘のトコは一人娘でね、つまり、私の　/690
孫なんだけど、その子が小学校に入ったんで、その世話を、私にさせたか
ったのよ。娘は仕事が大好きだけど、家庭と仕事の両立が難しくて、それ
で私を……。
【熊】そうなのか。ウチも、おっかぁに、見てもらってるんだよ。　/700

【マリ】熊さんトコも？　私、ここいらが、一人暮らしを止める潮時かな　　　/710
ぁって思ったんで、娘の意見に従ったの。だって、私、今、８８なのよ。
四捨五入したら、９０だわ。
【八】えっ、米寿だって！　どう見ても、５０そこそこだなぁ！　　　　　　/720
【マリ】まぁ、色男って、女を喜ばす言葉がスラスラと出るのねぇ。でも、　/730
そう言われると若返るわ。さぁ、二人とも、もっと飲んでね。
【八・熊】もう、腹がいっぱいだよ。それよりも、水泳の話をしようよ。　　/740
俺達、マリちゃんが、あんまり上手に泳ぐから、どうしたらあんなに泳げ
るのか知りたいんだ。マリちゃんは、昔、水泳の選手だったのかい。
【マリ】えっ、私が水泳の選手だったって？　とんでもない、水泳は５０　　/750
を過ぎて体が不自由になってから、医者に薦められて始めたのよ。ド素人
なのよ。
【八・熊】だけど、今は、速く泳ぐじゃないか。どうしてだい。　　　　　　/760
【マリ】私ね、どうしたら水泳が上手になるかなぁって考えて、それで、　　/770
思い切って試合に出てみようって決めたの。だって、みっともないのは嫌
だから、必死になって練習するでしょ。そうやったら、少しは上手になる
かなぁって。
【八・熊】俺達もそうなんだよ。いつもビリだけど、試合に出てるんだ。　　/780
【マリ】そうだったの。それを聞いて嬉しいわ。私は、それから、試合に　　/790
出る準備を始めたの。

【熊】準備って……どんな?　　　　　　　　　　　　　　　　　　　/800
【マリ】八つぁんも熊さんも、Tコーチを知っているでしょ。昼間だけの　/810
コーチだから、あまり会わないと思うけど、彼は、流体力学の専門家で、
それを使って、水泳の説明をしてくれるのよ。
【八・熊】流体力学?　それって難しくて、俺達なんかには、ムリだろ。　/820
【マリ】私も初めはそう思ったわ。でも、Tコーチの流体力学を使っての　/830
説明はとても分かりやすくて楽しかったの。それからは、彼の言う通りに
泳ぐようにしたらタイムも上がって、これなら試合に出てみようって……。
【熊】いいなぁ、マリちゃん、そんな説明を聞けて。俺達も、その水泳の　/840
流体力学とやらの説明、聞きたいなぁ。
【マリ】そうねぇ、そしたら、こうしたらどうかしら?　次からは、Tコ　/850
ーチもここに呼んで、一緒に飲みながら、話を聞くってのは。
【八】そりゃ、素晴らしいなぁ。マリちゃん、そのコーチと連絡とって、　/860
時間を決めてくれないか。俺達、8時過ぎなら、いつでもいいから。
【熊】それとどうだろう、定期的に話が聞けたら楽しいと思うんだ。例え　/870
ば月に1回ずつとか……。
【マリ】分かったわ。決まったら、連絡するわね。　　　　　　　　　　/880
【八】そうか……流体力学とやらを使って、水泳の説明をしてくれるのか。/890
マリちゃんに分かるんだから、俺にだって……。
【マリ】あら、八つぁん、何か言った?　　　　　　　　　　　　　　　/900
【八】あっ、いや、マリちゃんって、頭が良いなぁって……。　　　　　/910
【熊】八つぁん、ウチの社長がよく言うな、「人間は、頭も体もフル回転　/920
させないと、本当の健康生活とは言えない」って。俺達、ここんとこ、頭
を動かすことが不足してたと思うんだ。だから今度は、流体力学に挑戦し
て、頭と体の両方のバランスをとるようにしようよ。な、八つぁん、八つ
ぁんてば、聞いてるのかい?
【八】《独り言》そうか、俺が、流体力学なんて凄いことに挑戦してるっ　/930
て分かったら、カオリちゃん、たまげるぞー。「八つぁん、アタシにも、
その流体力学とやら、教えてね。近いうちに、ウチに来て、食事でもして、
その後で……」なんて言っちゃってさ!　そうだ、新しいネクタイ、買い
に行こ!　熊さん、色はやっぱり、ショッキング・ピンクかな?
【熊】????　　　　　　　　　　　　　　　　　　　　　　　　　　/940

---- 【終り】 ----

III. 《Rakugo》Hat-san・Kuma-san And Swimming Hydrodynamics

[11] A New Girlfriend

[Shigeko Hiraki]

------------------------(At the poolside)------------------------

【K】Today the swimming pool is very crowded... What lane will I swim in? Hey, Hat-san, Hat-san, what are you looking for?

【H】I'm searching for Kaori-chan... Can you see a girl in a gaudy bright pink bathing suit? Wow, there she is! She's swimming in lane two! Lots of other guys are swimming there already, I can't swim with her...

【K】Hat-san, why are you so upset? Anyone can swim in any lane! Oh, I see you want to watch her in the water, don't you?

【H】No, no... why would I be so impolite... Never...

【K】Hey, Hat-san, look at lane 4. That old woman "Hippo" is swimming there. She seems to be around 70, but she can swim very well, can't she?

【H】That's right. She's big and fat like a hippopotamus but can swim like a dolphin!

【K】Hat-san, I suppose she was a competition swimmer when she was younger...

【H】I think so too. It's no wonder that she can swim so well.

【K】Hat-san, how about we buy her some coffee and ask her why she can swim so well.

【H】That's a good idea. Let's chat to her and see if she's interested.

【K】Hat-san, she is not very young but she is surely a lady. As you are always good with the ladies, you try talking to her.

【H】Kuma-san, you always ask me to do that... Well, OK, I'll try. Excuse me, young lady! You can swim very well!

【Hippo】Thanks a lot! I'm very happy to hear that. OK, let's go for a drink at the pub nearby after swimming! I'll treat you to some beer.

【H】 Hey, hey, Kuma-san, I'm completely speechless. Help me and /250
continue the conversation.

【K】 Hat-san, if you can't do it, how can I do it? OK, OK, /260
I'll try. You said you'd treat us to some beer. That sounds
great! How about this? We'll meet at the pub in front of this
swimming pool at 8 p.m.

【Hippo】 That sounds great! I'm sure we'll have a good time /270
there. I'll treat you to some beer and you two handsome guys
can treat me to some good food. That's the deal, OK?

【H・K】 What?... /280

~~~~~~

【H】 It's the first time I've been to this pub. It's a pretty /290
good one. Nice to meet you. I'm Hachitaro. Call me Hat-san.

【K】 Nice to meet you! My name is Kumasuke. Call me /300
Kuma-san.

【Hippo】 OK. So on the left is Hat-san and on the right is /310
Kuma-san, right? Nice to meet the both of you too. My name is
Mari. Call me Mari-chan. Well, if we are all thirsty,
we should order beer first, eh? Hey, waiter, three big
glasses of beer, please.

【Waiter】 OK! Three big glasses of beer comming up! /320

【H】 Wow, I'm so thirsty... /330

【M】 OK, the both of you can sit over there and I'll sit here. /340
Because I'm so big and fat, I need a lot of room. When I was
young, tall girls were very rare and were stared at.

【K】 Oh... /350

【M】 But, I managed to meet my dear husband. He was smaller than /360
me but he said that he liked tall women. He sadly passed away
five years ago.

【H・K】 It sounds like you were happy... /370

【M】 When I was young my dream was to walk down the street /380
wearing high-heel shoes, but, I gave it up. On my birthday
he gave me a pair of red high-heel shoes. Oh, I was so happy
that I slept with the shoes next to my pillow...

【K】 You had a wonderful husband... /390

【M】 Oh, why did I talk to you about my husband... He looked /400
like Kuma-san and then I remembered him...

【Waiter】 Here is your beer. Would you like to order /410
something else?

【M】 I get very hungry after swimming so I'm going to order a lot /420
of delicious foods. Hat-san and Kuma-san, what do you want?

【H】 Hippo, oh, no, Mari-chan, please order something for us. /430

【M】 OK, hey, waiter! We'll have baked potatos with butter, /440
chicken kebabu, grilled herring with salt, baked eggplant,
pickles, rice balls... oh, I also want to order some ginkgo nuts
which are very good right now... Bring us everything I said.

【K】 It's too much for us... We can't eat it all... /450

【M】 It's OK. I have a container for the leftovers. I'll take /460
them home and have them for breakfast.

【H】 Wow, that's why you've become a "Hippo"... /470

【M】 What do you mean by "Hippo"? Is that your nickname /480
for me? I'm nervous about those words because I've been
called hog or hippopotamus, etc ever since I was a kid...

【H】 Oh, no, no... "Hippo" means Hippocrates. You know, /490
Hippocrates was a wonderful person in ancient Greece. So we use
it instead of wonderful. The word, "Hippocrates" is too long
so we use only "Hippo"...

【M】Wow, so we can use "Hippo" instead of the word "wonderful"? /500
I see. I'll write it down on my notebook and use it.
【H・K】What?... /510
【M】Hat-san, Kuma-san, now, let's give a toast to our /520
"wonderful" friendship, "Hippo"!
【H・K】Hip... hippo... /530
【H・K・M】<Glup, glup, glup> How delicious this beer is! /540
【Waiter】Hi! Here is your food. /550
【M】Let's have our food while it's still hot. The food tastes /560
good here, but unfortunately, it's expensive.
【H・K】What? Did you say it's expensive here? /570
【M】I'm kidding, it's a joke, of course. It's very cheap here. /580
Hat-san and Kuma-san, have as much food as you want.
【H】As much as we want?... but we have to pay for all /590
this food...
【M】What did you say? /600
【H】Nothing. Well, I'll have some chicken kebabu... /610
What is this? Only skewers left...
【M】Oh, I'm sorry, Hat-san. I've eaten all the chicken kababu. /620
Have some baked eggplant. It's also very good here.
【H】Wow, you've eaten it all? /630
【K】Never mind, Hat-san. The baked eggplant looks very tasty. /640
I'll have some ginkgo nuts... Wow, only the husks are left...
【M】Sorry, Kuma-san. I've eaten it all as well... /650
【K】It's OK, Mari-chan. I like the pickles the best. /660
By the way, is your house near here?
【M】Yes, it is. I had been living alone since my husband /670
passed away, but my daughter asked me to live with her.
【K】Very nice daughter! /680
【M】No, not at all. She has a daughter and she has just /690
entered elementary school. But, she can't manage both
the house-work and her own job. So, she asked me to live with
her and help her to take care of her daughter.
【K】My mom takes care of my son as well. She lives with us. /700

67

【M】 Same with me! I decided that I won't live alone because /710
I'm 88 years old now. If I round my age, I might be 90.

【H】 You are 88? You look 50 or so. /720

【M】 Wow, a handsome guy giving me compliments... I'm so happy /730
to hear them! Please drink up!

【H・K】 We've eaten and drunk enough. We are full. Now let's /740
talk about swimming. We wonder why you can swim so well.
Were you a swimming competitor when you were younger?

【M】 What? You're asking me if I was a swimming competitor? /750
Oh, no, no, I started to swim when I was 50 years old.
I started to swim because my health wasn't very good and
the doctor recommended it to me. I was a slow-swimmer.

【H・K】 Why can you swim so fast now? /760

【M】 I was thinking how I could swim faster and I found out the /770
best way. If I take part in a swimming competition, then I'll
improve my swimming skills because at the competition
I'd show that I'm a good swimmer.

【H・K】 We are the same. At the race we come in last /780
by a mile, but we take part in competitions always.

【M】 Really? I'm pleased to hear that. Now I'm practicing /790
for a competition.

【K】 Practicing for a competition? What do you mean? /800

【M】 You don't know T-coach, do you? He's the daytime swimming /810
coach here, so you won't see him. He is a specialist
in hydrodynamics. So he can talk about swimming using
that concept very well.

【H・K】 Hydrodynamics? It sounds too difficult for us? /820

【M】 At first I thought so as well. But his explanation was good /830
and enjoyable. Since then I tried to swim as he had taught me and,
it has improved my times. I decided to take part in a competiton.

【K】 It's very good that you've heard such a useful lecture /840
about swimming hydrodynamics. We also want to listen to him...

【M】 Well... How about this idea? We'll ask him to join us /850
in this pub. We'll listen to his lecture while we're drinking.

【H】That's a wonderful idea, Mari-chan! Contact him and /860
decide on the time, please. We are free every night after 8 p.m.
【K】And how about this... Ask him to teach us regularly. /870
For example, once a month...
【M】OK, I'll call you when the time has been decided. /880
【H】We'll learn hydro..something... I hope I can understand /890
it... but, if Mari-chan can understand it, I'm sure I can...
【M】What did you say, Hat-san? /900
【H】I..er...I just said Mari-chan is very understanding... /910
【K】Hat-san, our boss always says that people have to use /920
both brain and body energy together to lead a healthy life.
Our brains lack exercise, so, let's try to learn hydrodynamics
and thus, we'll use our brain energy too! Hey, Hat-san, Hat-san,
can you hear me?
【H】<soliloquy> Well, if Kaori-chan finds out I'm learning /930
such a difficult subject like hydrodynamics, she'll be very
impressed! She'll surely say, "Hat-san, Hat-san, please teach me
more about hydro... Come to my house for dinner and after
that...mmmm...." Oh, I must buy a new necktie... Kuma-san,
do you think the color should be a gaudy bright pink?!
【K】???? /940

---- 【END】 ----

[12]　ビオンディは何故負けた？　　　　　　　　　　　　　　　　　　　/100

〔平木 茂子（Shigeko Hiraki）〕

-------------------- （プールサイドのベンチで） --------------------　/110
【熊】八つぁん、カオリちゃんと、このベンチに座って、一体、何を話し　/120
てたんだよ。
【八】お、俺は、ゴ、ゴーグルを借りた礼を言っただけだぜ。　　　　　　/130
【熊】お前は、自分のゴーグルを水泳パンツの中に隠して、カオリちゃん　/140
に「ゴーグルを忘れたから貸してくれ」って言ってたな。俺は武士の情け
で、知らん顔をしてやったが、泳いだ後、お前のケツは、ゴーグルでこす
れて、真っ赤になってたじゃないか。俺、シャワー室で見たぞ。
【八】なんだって、熊さん、知ってて見逃してくれたっていうのかい？　　/150
【熊】当然だろ、武士の情けだもんな。　　　　　　　　　　　　　　　　/160
【八】フーン……。さーて、それじゃ行くか。Tコーチも、ドデカバちゃ　/170
んも、待たしちゃ悪いもんな。
【熊】八つぁん、彼女のこと、ドデカバとかドデカ・バーサンとか、絶対　/180
に呼ぶなよ。「ドデカバとは、ハッピーって意味だよ」って、何とか言い
逃れただろうが。忘れるな。
【八】分かってるってば、熊さん。　　　　　　　　　　　　　　　　　　/190

土手の河馬？

〜〜

　【マリ】八つぁーん、熊さーん、ここよー、ここ。待ってたのよー。　　/200
　【八・熊】マリちゃん、待たして、ゴメン。Ｔコーチは、まだかい。　　/210
　【マリ】「今、行きます」って連絡が入ったばかりよ。今日は、ドデカバ　/220
（ハッピー）な集まりになりそうね、そう思わない？
　【八・熊】そ、そ、そりゃ、そう思うよ……。　　　　　　　　　　　　/230
　【マリ】あら、いらしたわ。　　　　　　　　　　　　　　　　　　　　/240
　【Ｔコーチ】今晩は！　遅くなりました。　　　　　　　　　　　　　　/250
　【マリ】まぁ、Ｔコーチ、来てくださって、ありがとう。ご紹介します。　/260
こちらが、八つぁんと熊さんです。
　【八・熊】八と熊です。八つぁん、熊さんと呼んでください。よろしく。　/270
　【Ｔコーチ】こちらこそ、どーぞ、よろしく。僕は、八つぁんと熊さんの　/280
ことは、よく知っていますよ。何といっても、ウチのプールの有名人です
からね。
　【八】えっ、俺達が有名人？　何で？　　　　　　　　　　　　　　　　/290
　【Ｔコーチ】八つぁんも熊さんも、２５ｍを、何とか泳げるようになった　/300
時から、試合に出ているそうですね。僕、そんなファイトのある人、大好
きなんです。
　【熊】でも、いつも、圧倒的なビリなんです。　　　　　　　　　　　　/310
　【Ｔコーチ】「ビリでも出る」というその根性が立派だと思います。きっ　/320
と、素晴らしいスイマーになりますよ。
　【八・熊】いやー、Ｔコーチに、そんなこと言われると、嬉しいなぁ！　/330
　【マリ】ちょいと、お兄さーん、ここに、生ビールの大、４つ、持ってき　/340
て頂戴ね。
　【従業員】ハーイ、ただいま！　　　　　　　　　　　　　　　　　　　/350
　【マリ】Ｔコーチ、八つぁんと熊さんも、流体力学を使った水泳の説明を　/360
聞きたいそうなの。教えてあげてね。
　【Ｔコーチ】流体力学の説明を聞きたいとは、八つぁんも熊さんも、勉強　/370
家ですね。
　【熊】俺達、マリちゃんから、「Ｔコーチから、とても面白い水泳の流体　/380
力学の説明をしてもらった」って聞いたんです。それで俺達も、そんな話
が聞けたらなぁって。
　【Ｔコーチ】そうですか。僕の説明を聞きたいとは、嬉しいです。　　　/390
　【従業員】ビールと、おつまみ、お持ちしました。　　　　　　　　　　/400

71

【マリ】まー、美味しそう！　Ｔコーチも八つぁんも熊さんも、ドンドンやってちょうだいね。

【Ｔコーチ・八・熊】うわー、豪華版！　いただきまーす！

【Ｔコーチ】それじゃ、飲みながらやりましょう。皆さんは、ビオンディという水泳選手の名前を知っていますか？

【マリ】私は知っています。確か、ソウル・オリンピックの頃に活躍したアメリカの水泳選手でしょ。

【Ｔコーチ】その通りです。

【八】俺達は、その頃はまだ水泳を始めていなかったので、知りません。

【Ｔコーチ】そうですか。今日のタイトルは「ビオンディは何故負けた」です。ソウル・オリンピックの２００ｍ自由形で、絶対の本命と思われていたアメリカのビオンディ選手は、オーストラリヤのアームストロング選手に、タッチの差で逆転負けをしました。あれは、僕にとって、いまだに流体力学的な興味がいっぱいの試合です。

【マリ】その試合を、流体力学的に、説明してくださるのですか？

【Ｔコーチ】はい。昔から水泳の世界では、「試合の時は、隣の選手の少し後ろの位置につけて泳げ」と言われていました。

【八】それは、本当なんですか？

【Ｔコーチ】昔から言われていることは、経験から出ているので、現在の科学万能の世界でも通用することが多いのですが、流体力学が発達して、はっきりしてきたことが多々あります。これも、その１つで、色々な条件を満たした場合は、あり得ることではないかと、考えられています。

【熊】色々な条件とは、どんな条件ですか。

【Ｔコーチ】条件・その１は、横で泳ぐ人が自分より速いこと、その２は、横で泳ぐ人が、前半、急ピッチで泳いでくれること、その３は、その人が、自分のコース寄りで泳いでくれること、の３つが挙げられます。

【八・熊・マリ】ほぅ……。

【Ｔコーチ】皆さんは船などが進んでいる時に、船首から、先細りの三角形の波を引きずっているのを見たことがあると思いますが、このような波を、ケルビン波といいます。

【八・熊・マリ】ケルビン波？

【Ｔコーチ】はい。ケルビン波は、私達が泳いでいる時にも作られます。特に、上手な人が泳ぐと、その周りには綺麗なケルビン波が作られます。今度、プールの上から、観察してみてください。

【ケルビン波】

【ハ・熊・マリ】それは、是非、見なくっちゃ！ /580
【Tコーチ】試合の時に、貴方が隣のコースの選手の腰の辺りにぴったり /590
ついて泳いだとしたら、その選手の作るケルビン波、つまり、進行方向に
進む波に乗って泳ぐことになります。従ってその分、体力やキック力等を
セーブし、ラストに備えることが可能ではないかと、考えられています。
【ハ】すごく、トクするのですね。 /600
【Tコーチ】えぇ、リクツではそうですが、このような条件下で泳ぐこと /610
は、まず、ないと思うし、あったとしても、ビオンディ選手ぐらいの力の
あるスイマーでないと、ケルビン波の利用は出来ないでしょうね。
【マリ】ソウルでのあの試合に限って言えば、アームストロング選手が、 /620
ビオンディ選手に作戦勝ちをしたと考えて、よいのでしょうか。
【Tコーチ】そうですね、あの試合のビデオを見る限り、そう考えること /630
も可能です。しかし、すべては、流体力学的な推察に過ぎません。但し、
僕にとって、興味いっぱいの試合であったことだけは、確かです。
~~~~~~
【熊】さ、マリちゃん、遅くなったから、八つぁんと二人で送っていく /640
からね。バッグは俺が持つから、俺達の肩につかまるんだよ。

【マリ】まー、男性に送ってもらうなんて、何十年ぶりかしら。ワクワク　/650
するわ。

【八】もっと、しっかりつかまっていいんだよ。俺達、力なら、いくらで　/660
もあるんだ。いつも、重い物を持ち馴れているから、平気なんだ。

【マリ】二人とも優しいのね。こんな息子がいたら、年老いた親はどんな　/670
に幸せか……。八つぁん、熊さん、二人の子供時代の話を聞きたいわ。

【八】俺達に話すことなんか、ないんだよ。遊んでばっかりで、学校では　/680
いつも、ビリでさ……。

【マリ】でも、いつも二人、一緒だったんでしょ。　/690

【熊】ウン。二人とも、家が貧しかったから、助け合ってやってきたんだ。　/700
リンゴなんか、1個を半分ずつして、食べたんだよ。

【マリ】いいわねぇ、そんな友達同士……。あーら残念、もう着いちゃ　/710
ったわ。八つぁん、熊さん、ここが我が家なの。ハナコー、ただいまー。
私、ボーイ・フレンドに、送ってもらったの。ご挨拶、しなさーい！

【ハナコ（娘）】もー、お母さんったら、今、何時だと思ってんの。静か　/720
にしてよ。アララ、ホントに男性に送ってもらっちゃって……。申し訳、
ありません。いい歳して、いつも、こうなんですよ、ウチのドデカバは！

【八・熊・マリ】？ド、ドデカバ？……どうして、それを知って？　　　　　/730
【ハナコ】えっ、知ってたの？　いえね、いつも、ホロ酔い機嫌で帰って　　/740
来ては、玄関でドデーッと河馬のように引っくり返るんで、私、ドデカバ
ってあだ名をつけて、こっそり呼んでたんですよ。なーんだ、知ってたの
か。それならば、これからはお母さんじゃなくて、ドデカバって呼びます
からね。あー、スカッとするわ！
【マリ】えっ、何ですって、ハナコ、私のこと、ドデカバって呼びたいっ　　/750
て、それホント？　そうだったの、私と一緒にいると、そんなにドデカバ
（ハッピー）だったなんてねぇ！　ハナコー、アンタだって、私のドデカ
バなのよ！

----【終り】----

-------------------------------【参考資料】-------------------------------
◆（選手・コーチ・中高年スイマーのための）楽しい・水泳の流体力学
　平木茂子・竹島良憲・今井恒雄・他著／恒星社厚生閣／1994
◆（やさしい流体力学を覚えよう）生活の中の楽しい水泳
　平木茂子・今井恒雄・竹島良憲・上原五百枝・他著／恒星社厚生閣／1998
◆（落語を使って英語・日本語を学ぼう）英語落語・日本語落語　大集合！
　平木茂子・今井恒雄・上原五百枝・根尾延子・テーラー、マーク・マクアリア、マーク・他著／
　恒星社厚生閣／2004／日・英対訳

[12] Why Biondi Lost?

[Shigeko Hiraki]

------------------(On the bench at the pool side)------------------
【K】Hat-san, what were you talking about with Kaori-chan while you were sitting on the bench together?
【H】I, I only said, "Thanks for lending me your goggles".
【K】You hid your goggles in your swimming costume and told Kaori-chan that you had forgotten them. Then you said to her "Can I borrow yours?". While we were taking our showers, I noticed the red mark on your bottom from where you had hid your goggles.
【H】Kuma-san, you were spying on me, weren't you?
【K】Of course. We are friends and we must help each other.
【H】Thanks, Kuma-san. Now, let's go. It's not good if T-coach and Hippo have to wait for us at the pub.
【K】Hat-san, never call her "Hippo". We told her that "Hippo" means "wonderful" though... Remember!
【H】I know, I know, Kuma-san.

【M】 Hi! Hat-san, Kuma-san, I'm here! Come on over here! /200
I'm waiting for you!

【H・K】 Mari-chan, we are so sorry to keep you waiting. /210
How about T-coach?

【M】 He just called me and said he'd come soon. I'm sure /220
that today's meeting will be a very "Hippo" one. Dont'you
think so?

【H・K】 O...O...Of course, we think so too... /230

【M】 Oh, here he is now. /240

【T-coach】 Good evening, everyone! Sorry to be late. /250

【M】 Oh, T-coach! Thanks for coming! I'll introduce you /260
to Hat-san and Kuma-san.

【H・K】 I'm Hachi. I'm Kuma. Call us Hat-san and kuma-san. /270
Nice to meet you!

【T-coach】 Nice to meet you too! I know Hat-san and Kuma-san /280
very well because you are famous among the coaches.

【H】 What? You say we are famous? Why? /290

【T-coach】 Both of you have taken part in the swimming /300
competitions since you could barely swim 25 meters,
haven't you? I like such fighting spirits as yours!

【K】 But... we always came in last by a mile. /310

【T-coach】 You both will be great swimmers because you don't /320
mind taking any result you receive.

【H・K】 Wow, praise from T-coach! You've made us very happy! /330

【M】 Hey, waiter, bring us four big glasses of beer, please. /340

【Waiter】 Sure. /350

【M】 T-coach, Hat-san and Kuma-san want to learn swimming /360
hydrodynamics from you. Please teach it to them as well.

【T-coach】 It's admirable that the both of you are so studious, /370
and that you want to learn about swimming hydrodynamics.

【K】 Mari-chan told us that you had talked about swimming /380
hydrodynamics with her. We'd like you to explain it to us
as well, please!

【T-coach】 I see. Then I'll be pleased to do that. /390

【Waitor】Your beer and some snacks are ready.　Here you are.　　　　/400
【M】Wow, it looks good!　　　　/410
【T-coach・H・K】Hmmmm...　It looks so delicious!　　　　/420
【T-coach】Now let's start while we're drinking and eating.　　　　/430
Do you know the name "Biondi"?
【M】Yes, I do.　He was a great American swimmer around the time　　/440
of the Seoul Olympics, wasn't he?
【T-coach】That's right.　　　　/450
【H】We don't know him because we hadn't started to swim then.　　　/460
【T-coach】I see.　Today's theme is, "Why Biondi lost?".　　　　/470
At the Seoul Olympics, Biondi lost the 200 meters free style to
an Australian swimmer, Armstrong.　Biondi was thought to surely
win but he lost at the very last moment.　For me, that race is
the most interesting one as a researcher in hydrodynamics.
【M】You'll explain that race to us from a hydrodynamics　　　　/480
point of view, won't you?
【T-coach】Yes.　Since old times, swimmers have been taught that　　/490
during the race they should swim following the swimmer in the next
lane.　[your head should be positioned level with the hip of
the swimmer in the next lane.]
【H】Is it true?　　　　/500
【T-coach】Old proverbs, colloquial expressions and legends are　　　/510
passed down from experience, and some of them are worthy in the
modern scientific world.　Nowadays, hydrodynamics has progressed
and many unknown things have been cleared up.　"Swim following
the swimmer in the next lane" is one of them.　It's thought that
if several conditions are fulfilled it might be true.
【K】What are those several conditions?　　　　/520
【T-coach】Condition No.1 is that the swimmer in the next lane　　　/530
should be faster than you.　No.2 is that the swimmer in the next
lane should swim using full energy from the beginning.　No.3
is that the swimmer in the next lane should swim near to you
in his own lane.
【H・K・M】Interesting...　　　　/540

【T-coach】 Have you seen the triangular taper wave that a ship /550
makes while moving? This is called the Kelvin wave.

【H・K・M】 The Kelvin wave? /560

【T-coach】 Yes. Not only a ship, but also a swimmer can make /570
the Kelvin wave while swimming. If the swimmer swims very fast,
obviously the Kelvin wave would be seen. Next time check it out
on the second floor of our pool.

【H・K・M】 We will! /580

【T-coach】 If you swim following the swimmer in the next lane, /590
you can use the Kelvin wave's power [going forward power]
made by the next swimmer. By doing this, you can save your
energy, kicking power and so on until the last moment.

【H】 Wow, it's a great technique! /600

【T-coach】 Yes. But such a lucky condition as this /610
almost never happens. If you had conditions like this,
the next swimmer would have to be as powerful as Biondi.
So, it's hardly ever occurs.

[The Kelvin Wave]

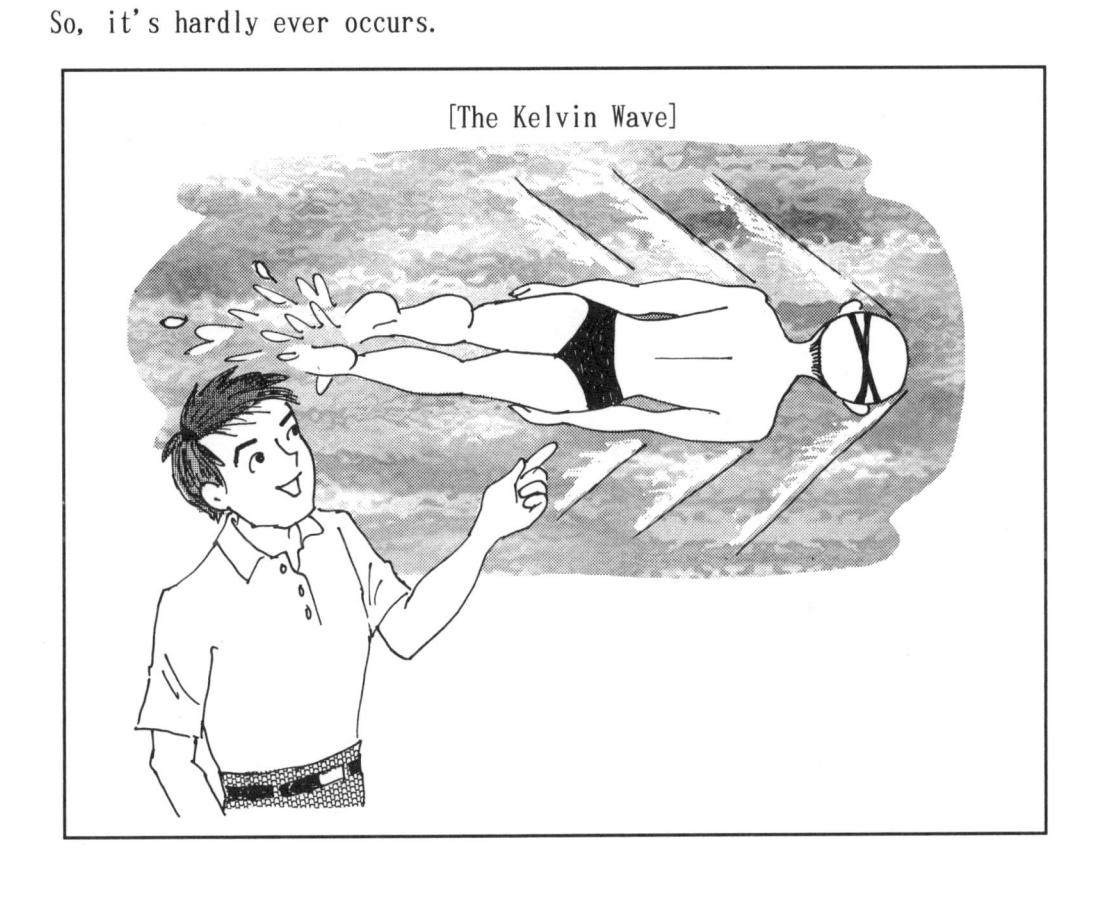

【M】At the Seoul Olympics, the Australian swimmer, Armstrong, /620
beat Biondi using good tactics like these... I mean, Armstrong
used the Kelvin effect to his own advantage, didn't he?

【T-coach】Well, as I watch the video of the race, I could say /630
that your opinion is probably right.　But I'm only inferring
this from hydrodynamics.　Anyway, for me the most interesting
race is from a swimming hydrodynamics point of view.

~~~~~~

【K】Hey, Mari-chan!　Hat-san and I will see you home. /640
I'll carry your bag, so hang on to our shoulders.

【M】How nice that two charming guys will see me home! /650
I haven't had such an experience like this for a long, long
time...　I'm so excited!

【H】Hold our shoulders more tightly.　We are really strong /660
because we are used to moving heavy things at our job.

【M】How kind of the both of you!　If all parents had such sons /670
like you, how happy they'd be...　Hat-san, Kuma-san, tell me
the stories of your childhood.　I'd love to hear them.

【H】 Well, there's not much to talk about ourselves. We played /680
all the time and we were always at the bottom of the class.

【M】 But, were you always doing this together?... /690

【K】 Yeah. We were so poor that we had to help each other. /700
We would even share an apple between us.

【M】 I envy your friendship... Wow, we're here! Hat-san /710
and Kuma-san, this is my home. Hi, Hanako, my boyfriends
have seen me home. Come here and greet them.

【Hanako(daughter)】 Hey, mom, do you know what time it is now? /720
Be quiet. Wow, it's true that your boyfriends saw you home...
Oh, I'm sorry to bother you, guys! Thanks for escorting
my mother, "Hippo" home.

【H・K・M】 How do you know that word... "Hippo"? /730

【Hanako】 What? You all know her nickname, "Hippo"? /740
Young guys, my mom always drinks when she comes home and then
lies on her back at the entrance just like a hippopotamus.
Well, as everyone knows your nickname, I'll call you hippo
instead of mom, anytime, anywhere, always...

【M】 What? Hanako, You want to call me, "Hippo"? Wow I never /750
knew you felt so wonderful to have me live with you!
It's so great, that I have such a hippo... I mean wonderful
daughter like you!

---- 【END】 ----

------------------ 【 Reference : Author's own works 】 ----------------
◆— For competitor, coach, middle-aged swimmer — Enjoy swimming
   hyderodynamics (by) Shigeko Hiraki/Yoshinori Takeshima/Tsuneo Imai
   & others. Koseisyakoseikaku/1994/In Japanese
◆— Let's learn hydrodynamics — Enjoyable swimming in daily life
   (by) Shigeko Hiraki/Tsuneo Imai/Yoshinori Takeshima/Ioe Uehara &
   others. Koseisyakoseikaku/1998/In Japanese
◆A Big Selection Of Rakugo In English And Japanese! (By) Shigeko Hiraki
   /Tsuneo Imai/Ioe Uehara/Nobuko Neo/Mark Taylor/Mark McAlear & others.
   Koseisyakoseikaku/2004/In English & Japanese

[13] ゴーグルは何故外れる？ /100

〔平木 茂子 (Shigeko Hiraki)〕

------------------------ (シャワー室で) ------------------------ /110
【八】熊さん、そこの石鹸、取ってくれないか。 /120
【熊】はいよ、ほおるぜ。ところで、お前の今日の水泳パンツ、凄え派手 /130
だったけど……いくら何でも、ショッキング・ピンクって色は、八つぁん
には……。
【八】いかすだろ。あれは、この前の日曜日に、商店街のバーゲンで買っ /140
たんだ。色で決めたんだよ。
【熊】あれ、腰の辺りがブカついてて、何だかバーサンの……。 /150
【八】「何だかバーサン」って何だよ。熊さんには、あの色とデザインの /160
良さは分かんないよ。そりゃ少しは大きいけど、1枚しか残ってなかった
からなぁ……。可愛いあの子の水着と、お揃いの色だぜ。
【熊】「可愛いあの子」って誰だい。そうか、今度は、カオリちゃんだな。 /170
又々、ふられるってのに、懲りないなぁ。
【八】熊さん、何か言ったかい。じゃ、俺、先に行ってるぜ。 /180

【Tコーチ】それじゃ、飲みながら説明しますね。今日は、「ゴーグルは /190
何故外れる」をやりましょう。

【八】そりゃ、いいなぁ！ 俺達、飛び込むたびに、ゴーグルが外れてし /200
まうんで、試合の時はつけないんです。

【熊】時には、ゴーグルが鼻の上にかぶさって、苦しくて……。 /210

【Tコーチ】そうですか。それでは、これから説明することに注意して、 /220
飛び込みの練習を、してみてください。

【八・熊・マリ】はい。 /230

【八】Tコーチ、熊さんがノートに書きますから、ゆっくりお願いします。 /240

【Tコーチ】分かりました。飛び込みの際に、ゴーグルが外れないように /250
するためには、アゴを引いておく必要があります。アゴを引いていないと、
ゴーグルは外れます。これを、しっかり頭に入れておいてください。

【マリ・八・熊】分かりました。 /260

【Tコーチ】アゴを出して飛び込むと、ゴーグルの位置に水が当たります。 /270
その勢いで、ゴーグルが外れるので……。

【八】分かった！ 水がゴーグルに当たらないように飛び込めば、ゴーグ /280
ルは、外れないんだ！

【Tコーチ】その通りです。アゴを引けばゴーグルに水は当たらず、むし /290
ろ、後頭部の辺りに当たります。

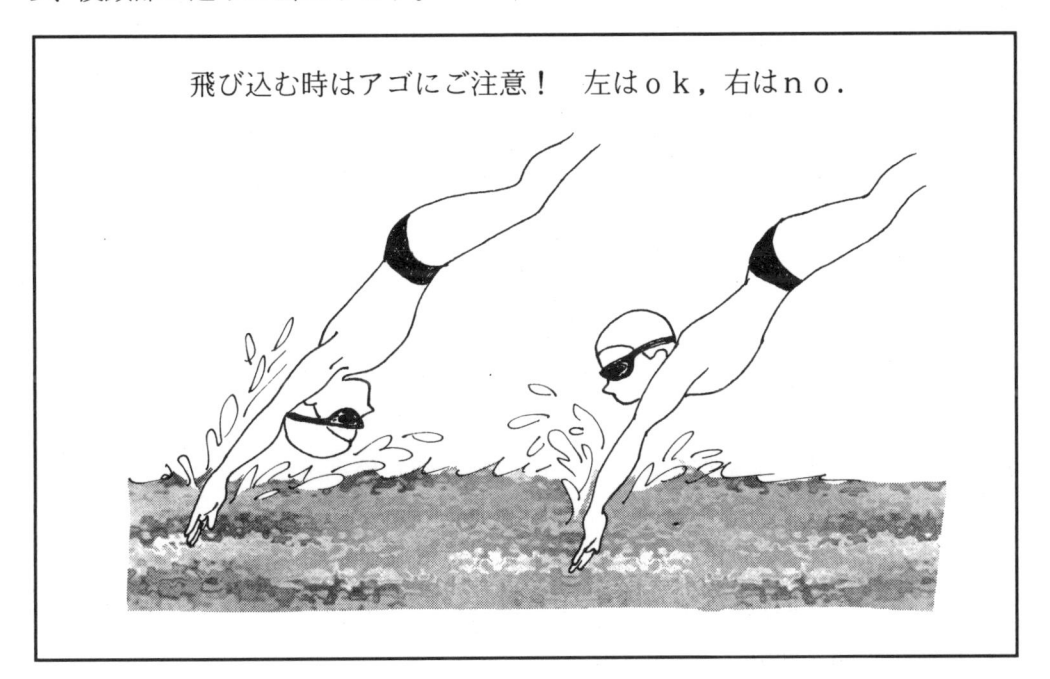

飛び込む時はアゴにご注意！ 左はｏｋ，右はｎｏ．

【八】そうかー、簡単なんだな。　　　　　　　　　　　　　　　　　/300
【Ｔコーチ】理屈は簡単ですが、初心者のうちは、アゴを引いた形には、/310
なかなか、なりません。
【熊】自分では、アゴを引いたつもりでも、実際には、そうなってないっ/320
てことですか。
【Ｔコーチ】その通りです。アゴを引いたつもりでも、一番重要な入水の/330
時点で、瞬間的にアゴを出してしまうんですね。
【マリ】そう、そうなるわ……。　　　　　　　　　　　　　　　　/340
【Ｔコーチ】しっかりアゴを引くと、水は後頭部に当たり、顔からアゴに/350
かけて水の流れが体から離れ、渦が出来るのです。ゴーグルをこの渦の
中に入れてしまえば、ゴーグルは外れません。
【マリ】ゴーグルの外れるワケは、これだけですか？　　　　　　　/360
【Ｔコーチ】気をつける点は、他にもありますが、それは１００分の１秒/370
を争うような選手の場合です。このような場合には、あまりアゴを引き過
ぎると、後頭部の抵抗が増し、その分、タイムが遅くなることがあり得る
かも知れません。しかし、中高年者の場合は、「アゴを出さなければゴー
グルは外れない」と考えていいでしょう。
【熊】よく分かりました。早速、練習してみます。今日は、俺達が、一番/380
困っていたことを、分かりやすく説明してもらって、嬉しかったです。
【Ｔコーチ】今度、皆さんの練習を見に行きますね。頑張ってください。/390
【八】よーし、これでもう、ゴーグルは外れないぞ。今後は、飛び込む/400
時には、「アゴを出すな」って、肝に命じて……。
【熊】八つぁんよ、お前の場合は、「アゴを出すな・手も出すな」だろ。/410

----【終り】----

------------------------------【参考資料】------------------------------

◆（選手・コーチ・中高年スイマーのための）楽しい・水泳の流体力学
　　平木茂子・竹島良憲・今井恒雄・他著／恒星社厚生閣／1994
◆（やさしい流体力学を覚えよう）生活の中の楽しい水泳
　　平木茂子・今井恒雄・竹島良憲・上原五百枝・他著／恒星社厚生閣／1998
◆（落語を使って英語・日本語を学ぼう）英語落語・日本語落語　大集合！
　　平木茂子・今井恒雄・上原五百枝・根尾延子・テーラー、マーク・マクアリア、マーク・他著／
　　恒星社厚生閣／2004／日・英対訳

[13] Why Goggles Come Off When Diving?

[Tsuneo Imai]

---------------------- (In the shower-room) ----------------------

【H】 Kuma-san, pass me the soap.

【K】 OK, I'll toss it to you. By the way, today, your swimming trunks are too flowery. That gaudy pink color does't suit you.

【H】 It's cool, isn't it? I bought it last Sunday at a sale at a shopping mall. I decided to buy it because of the color.

【K】 And, it's too big for you. It's something like a pair of bloomers for Mother.

【H】 How do you mean by, "for Mother"? You don't appreciate the color and the design of it? It's true that It's a little bit large for me, but it was the only one left in stock. A cute girl I fancy and I have got matching swimwear of the same colour.

【K】 Who's that "cute girl". Gotcha! So, Your cute new girl is Kaori, isn't she? You weren't lucky in love were you? You never learn, do you?

【H】 Kuma-san, did you say something about me? Now, I'm going to go to the pub alone.

~~~~~~

【T-coach】 Now, I will explain the reason why our goggles come off while we are drinking together.

【H】 It's cool! Goggles are always coming off when we start and dive into the pool, so we don't use goggles at competitions anymore.

【K】 So many times, our goggles would hang over our nose and therefore we couldn't breath well.

【T-coach】 I know. Well, I'll explain to you how to dive into a pool properly. If you understand what I say, you will be able to do it well.

【H・K・M】 OK.

【H】 T-coach, Kuma-san writes down what you say, so could you explain it slowly enough for us to follow.

【T-coach】I see. Draw your chin in, so that your goggles don't /250
come off when diving. If you don't draw your chin in, your goggles
will come off. Keep this in mind.

【H・K・M】We understand. /260

【T-coach】If you dive sticking out your chin, streams of water /270
will catch your goggles and they will come off.

【H】I understand very well! The streams will not catch the /280
goggles when the chin is not sticking out.

【T-coach】Quite so. The chin doesn't stick out, the stream /290
doesn't catch the goggles. The stream catches more the back of
the head rather than the goggles.

【H】I see... It's very simple reason. /300

【T-coach】Right. It isn't difficult, but the beginner can't do /310
it easily.

【K】It means that trying to do so makes it difficult for the /320
beginner, doesn't it.

【T-coach】So it is. They try to draw the chin in, but they stick /330
out the chin at the moment of diving.

[Position of your chin when diving : Left is ok, right is no]

【M】 Yes. I also try to do so, but I can't. /340

【T-coach】 When you draw the chin in, the stream catches more the /350 back of the head and comes off your face and your chin. Rather, it makes a whirl of water under the chin. If you can keep your goggles in while the water is whirling, your goggles won't come off.

【M】 Is that the only reason why our goggles come off when diving? /360

【T-coach】 There are other points of course, but, they are for /370 swimmers who compete at the top level to one-hundredth of a second. In such a case, if they draw the chin in too much, water resistance will increase and swimming speed will slow down. But, middle-aged people have to concentrate on,"If you draw your chin in, your goggles will not come off".

【K】 We understand very well. We'll practice it right away. /380 We are very happy to hear about how we can solve the problem of our goggles coming off when diving. It's our biggest problem.

【T-coach】 I'll visit your practice session in the near future. /390 Do your best!

【H】 Well, I now know how to dive without my goggles coming off. /400 I'll take "drawing the chin" to heart.

【K】 Hat-san, in your case, it's "Keep your chin in and keep your /410 hands in your pockets!"

---- 【END】 ----

------------------ 【 Reference : Author's own works 】 ----------------

◆— For competitor, coach, middle-aged swimmer — Enjoy swimming hyderodynamics (by) Shigeko Hiraki/Yoshinori Takeshima/Tsuneo Imai & others. Koseisyakoseikaku/1994/In Japanese

◆— Let's learn hydrodynamics — Enjoyable swimming in daily life (by) Shigeko Hiraki/Tsuneo Imai/Yoshinori Takeshima/Ioe Uehara & others. Koseisyakoseikaku/1998/In Japanese

◆A Big Selection Of Rakugo In English And Japanese! (By) Shigeko Hiraki /Tsuneo Imai/Ioe Uehara/Nobuko Neo/Mark Taylor/Mark McAlear & others. Koseisyakoseikaku/2004/In English & Japanese

[14]　タイムアップはこれでバッチリ！　　　　　　　　　　　/100

〔平木　茂子（Shigeko Hiraki）〕

------------------------（プールの会議室で）------------------------　　/110
　【Ｔコーチ】やー、皆さん、ようこそ！　今回は、昼から、ウチの会議室　/120
でやろうということだったので、お茶を用意しておきました。ほら、いい
香りでしょ。これ、静岡の友人が送ってくれたんです。
　【マリ】まぁ、Ｔコーチ、ありがとう。私は、お弁当を作ってきましたよ。　/130
孫娘が手伝ってくれたんです。
　【八】俺、コーヒーを沸かして、ポットに詰めてきました。俺のコーヒー　/140
は、日本一なんです。
　【熊】俺は、オヤツに焼き芋を持ってきました。子供の頃は、こればっか　/150
りだったんで、懐かしくて。
　【Ｔコーチ】凄いじゃないですか、こんなに色々と！　僕、お腹が、ペコ　/160
ペコなんです。
　【マリ】それじゃ、まず、食べてから始めましょうね。さ、どーぞ。　　　/170
　【全員】いただきまーす！　《ムシャムシャ・ガブガブ》あー、旨い！　　/180
　【マリ】あら、アッと言う間に、空っぽだわ。よかったー！　　　　　　　/190
　【Ｔコーチ】あー、美味しかった！　それに、このコーヒーも抜群ですね。　/200
　【熊】ウチの会社じゃ、それ、「八つぁんの元気の出るコーヒー」って呼　/210
んでるんです。社長も大好きなんですよ。
　【マリ】どうしたら、こんなに美味しく入れられるのか、教えて欲しいわ。　/220
　【八】マリちゃんなら、喜んで、ヒミツの入れ方、教えますよ。　　　　　/230
　【Ｔコーチ】さーて、コーヒーで元気が出たところで、始めましょうか。　/240

【八・熊・マリ】ハーイ、お願いします。
【Tコーチ】今日のテーマは、「タイムアップを目指そう」です、期待してください。
【八】いいなぁ！　それじゃ、熊さん、ノートの方、がっちり頼むぜ。
【熊】又……。こういうことは、いつだって俺なんだから……。
【Tコーチ】いつも、熊さんが、ノートをとる係なんですか？
【熊】ガキの頃から、ずーっとなんです。
【八】でも、体を使うことは、ぜーんぶ、俺がやってるから。
【Tコーチ】いいなぁ、そんな友達同士って！　僕、羨ましいです。
【マリ】そうなのよ。見ていて、私にもそんな友達がいたら、どんなに、嬉しいかなぁって……。
【八・熊】照れちゃうよ。俺達なんかのことじゃなくて、流体力学の話を始めてください。
【Tコーチ】そうしましょう。今日のテーマの「タイムアップを目指そう」ですが、別の言い方をすると、「アゴを引いて泳ごう」です。又々、アゴが問題になります。アゴは、何をやるにしても重要かも知れませんね。
【熊】この前の「ゴーグルが外れる」も、「アゴを出す」が原因だったからなぁ。
【Tコーチ】えぇ。あれも、今日の話に関係しています。
【八】アゴは、水泳のイノチなのかな。
【Tコーチ】そうなんですよ。水泳では、飛び込む時だけでなく、4つの泳法のどれでも、アゴを引いて泳ぐ必要があります。その理由を、背泳の例で説明します。
【マリ】まぁ、私、背泳が大好きだから、嬉しいわ。
【Tコーチ】背泳では水面に対して、出来るだけ真っ直ぐな姿勢をとることが理想です。アゴを出してしまう、つまり、上を向き過ぎると、アゴの下にくぼみが出来て、水がスムーズに流れなくなり、渦が出来、これが、スピードを落とす原因になります。
【マリ】「くぼみ」がスピードを落とす……。
【Tコーチ】くぼみがあると、水は、アゴの下から喉に流れ込もうとして、そこで、急激な方向転換をします。流れの性質として、急激な方向転換をすると、流れが物体、例えば、私達の体の表面をスムーズに流れなくなり渦が発生します。この渦がアゴの下流の流れの速度を落とします。流体力学では、この速度が落ちた流れのことを、ウエーク（WAKE）と言います。

【マリ】ゴーグルが外れないようにするためには、渦を作って、その中に　　/440
ゴーグルを入れて、外れないようにするのでしたね。これは、速度の落ち
た渦を利用しているケースですね。

【Tコーチ】はい、よく覚えていましたね。　　　　　　　　　　　　　　/450

【熊】泳ぐ時は、その逆で、体を出来るだけ真っ直ぐにして、渦が出来な　/460
いようにしないと、いけないのですね。

【Tコーチ】そうです。例えば、背中を曲げてもソンをすると考えてくだ　/470
さい。中高年者は、くぼみのある・渦を作る姿勢を作らないことに注意す
るだけで、ムリなく綺麗で速い泳ぎになります。私の言う「速く泳ごう」
とは、こうやってタイムを上げることです。

【八】ひゃ……、いいこと教わっちゃたー！　これで、タイムはバッチリ、/480
カオリちゃんと並んで泳げるぞ！　ナニも、バッチリだなー！

【Tコーチ】……八つぁん、申し訳ないんですが、カオリは、僕のワイフ　/490
なんです……。

---- 【終り】 ----

------------------------------【参考資料】------------------------------

◆（選手・コーチ・中高年スイマーのための）楽しい・水泳の流体力学
　平木茂子・竹島良憲・今井恒雄・他著／恒星社厚生閣／1994
◆（やさしい流体力学を覚えよう）生活の中の楽しい水泳
　平木茂子・今井恒雄・竹島良憲・上原五百枝・他著／恒星社厚生閣／1998
◆（落語を使って英語・日本語を学ぼう）英語落語・日本語落語　大集合！
　平木茂子・今井恒雄・上原五百枝・根尾延子・テーラー､マーク・マクアリア､マーク・他著／
　恒星社厚生閣／2004／日・英対訳

[14] The Secret Of How To Swim Faster!

[Tsuneo Imai]

---------------- (In a meeting room of a sport gym) ----------------

【T-coach】 Hi! Welcome. We've decided to have our next meeting this afternoon at our gym, so I have prepared Japanese tea for you. It smells sweet, doesn't it? My friend living in Shizuoka prefecture sent it to me.

【Mari】 T-coach, thanks. I have cooked our lunch box, and my granddaughter helped me.

【H】 I made some coffee for us, and I have brought it inside a thermos flask. I can brew coffee very well.

【K】 I have brought some baked potatoes for our tea break. I always had them for tea break in my childhood. It brings back old memories for me.

【T-coach】 Oh, these preparations are great! I feel so hungry.

【M】 OK! Let's take our lunch. Here you are.

【Members】 Let's eat! <chomp, chomp, guzzle, guzzle> It's great!

【M】 Ah! It's already empty. I'm very happy!

【T-coach】 Yeah, delicious! And the coffee was also tasty.

【K】 We called it, "the cheering up coffee of Hat-san". Our boss also loves it.

【M】 I want to know how to brew such a sweet coffee.

【H】 Mari-chan. I'll be pleased to teach you how to brew it.

【T-coach】 Nooww! We feel refreshed after the coffee, so let's start to learn about today's theme.

【H・K・M】 OK. Please start the lesson for us.

【T-coach】 Today's theme is, "how to swim faster". You might have expected it?

【H】 I'd like to do so! Now, Kuma-san, are you ready to write down T-coach's explanation.

【K】 Yet again. I always have to write it down ...

【T-coach】 Do you always take notes of what you hear?

【K】 Yes, we have always done so since our childhood. /300

【H】 That's right, but I take charge of other work. /310
For example, brewing coffee or arranging a meeting room.

【T-coach】 That's a good relationship! I admire it. /320

【M】 I think so too. I would also like to have such a friend. /330

【H・K】 It's embarrassing for us. Please start the lecture of /340
hydrodyanmics.

【T-coach】 OK! Today's theme is, "How to swim faster", but we /350
need to take a new view of the matter, in light of "Don't stick
your chin out when you swim". Yet again, the chin is the main
subject. The chin is important in various ways.

【K】 So, the last theme, "why our goggles come off" is related to /360
"sticking out the chin".

【T-coach】 Yes. That is related to today's theme. /370

【H】 The chin is important when swimming. /380

【T-coach】 That's right. It's very important in swimming to /390
draw your chin in, not only for diving but also for each four
styles of swimming. For example, I'll explain it when you swim
the back stroke style.

【M】 Oh, I'm pleased because I love the back stroke style. /400

【T-coach】 In the case of back stroke, it's ideal to keep your /410
body as straight as possible on a line parallel with the
surface. When you look ahead too much, your chin will stick
out and currents of water will flow into the pit below your chin.
It will make a whirl of water in the pit
and your swimming speed will slow
down. This whirl is an example
of water resistance.

【M】 The pit below /420
our chin causes
our swimming
speed to
slow
down.

92

【T-coach】 Good. Water will flow along the surface of your body. /430
If the surface isn't calm, the water stream will shoot upwards off
the surface of your body, and it will make a whirl of water in the
pit. This whirl will cause your swimming speed to slow down. We
call this effect,"WAKE" in hydrodyanmics.

【M】 The stream won't flow to the inside of the chin and it will /440
make a whirl of water under the chin. If we can keep our goggles
in the whirl, our goggles won't come off. It's a hightly
effective way of using the whirl, isn't it.

【T-coach】 That's right. You remember it well, don't you. /450

【K】 When we want to swim faster, we have to keep our body in a /460
straight line, so as not to make the whirl, don't we?

【T-coach】 Yes. For example, you had better take care not to /470
bend your back to swim faster. If you swim with your body
straight, you can swim faster and more natural. My motto,
"swimming faster" means the method I have just explained.

【H】 Wow... This is it! Thank heavens! It's sure that I will /480
be able to swim faster now with Kaori-chan by my side. I'm also
sure to fulfill my dream!

【T-coach】 Hat-san, I'm sorry, Kaori is my wife... /490

---- 【END】 ----

----------------- 【 Reference : Author's own works 】 ---------------
◆─ For competitor, coach, middle-aged swimmer ─ Enjoy swimming
   hyderodynamics (by) Shigeko Hiraki/Yoshinori Takeshima/Tsuneo Imai
   & others. Koseisyakoseikaku/1994/In Japanese
◆─ Let's learn hydrodynamics ─ Enjoyable swimming in daily life
   (by) Shigeko Hiraki/Tsuneo Imai/Yoshinori Takeshima/Ioe Uehara &
   others. Koseisyakoseikaku/1998/In Japanese
◆A Big Selection Of Rakugo In English And Japanese! (By) Shigeko Hiraki
   /Tsuneo Imai/Ioe Uehara/Nobuko Neo/Mark Taylor/Mark McAlear & others.
   Koseisyakoseikaku/2004/In English & Japanese

[15] バッチャーンはダメよ！　　　　　　　　　　　　　　　　/100

〔平木 茂子（Shigeko Hiraki）〕

------------------------（練習が終わって）------------------------ /110
【熊】八つぁん、コーチやマリちゃんを待たしちゃ悪いから、急いでシャ /120
ワーを浴びて、行こうぜ。
【八】ウン。今日は、Tコーチが、友達のコーチを連れてくるって言って /130
たな。あれれー、チャンス到来だ！
【熊】八つぁん、急ごうってば。何、キョロキョロしてるんだよ。 /140
【八】熊さん、ホレ、4コースで泳いでいる人、上手いなぁ。 /150
見てみろよ。あっ、ドスーン。
【モモエ】きゃー！　誰か、助けてー！ /160
【八】あっ、モモエちゃん！　危ない！　さぁ、俺の手につかまるんだよ。 /170
よいしょっと。あれ、小指が赤くなってる。ゴメン、ゴメンよ。
【モモエ】まぁ、八つぁんだったの。私、泳げないから、びっくりしちゃ /180
ったわ。でも、大丈夫よ。
【八】熊さん、先に行っててくれよ。俺、モモエちゃんを、医務室に連れ /190
ていくからさ。
【熊】モモエちゃんなら「大丈夫」って言っただろ。八つぁんよ、お前、 /200
わざと彼女にぶつかったな。俺、ちゃんと、見てたんだぞ。泳いでいる人
を見ているフリをして、段々、後ずさりしていったじゃないか。
【八】しーっ、声が大きいよ。あー、熊さんさえ、いなけりゃ、いいセン、 /210
いってたのになぁ……。

～～～～～～～～～～～～～～～～～～～～～～～～～～～～～～～～～～

【Tコーチ】遅くなりました。紹介します。友人のYコーチです。彼も、流体力学の専門家なんですよ。

【Yコーチ】初めまして、よろしく。

【八・熊・マリ】こちらこそ、よろしく。

【Yコーチ】僕は、Tコーチから皆さんのことを聞いて、羨ましく思っていたのですよ。とても、研究熱心だそうですね。

【八】いやー、それほどでも……しかし、学ぶってことは、確かに……。

【熊】八つぁん、何、恰好つけてんだよ。Yコーチ、俺達は、Tコーチの水泳の流体力学の説明がとっても楽しいので、一生懸命、聞いているだけなんです。

【マリ】さぁ、食べながら、やりましょうね。鍋の季節だから、トリ鍋を注文しておきました。飲み物を頼んでと……お兄さーん、ここに、生ビールの大、5つ、お願い。それで、Tコーチ、今日のテーマは何ですか。

【Tコーチ】今日は、折角、Yコーチに来てもらったので、彼に話をしてもらおうと思っているのですよ。

【マリ】まぁ、そうですか。それで、Yコーチ、何の話をしてくださるのですか。

【Yコーチ】そうですね、ターンについて説明しようと思って用意してきましたが、このテーマでは、いかがですか。

【八・熊・マリ】わー、いいなぁ。三人とも、この間から、クイック・ターンの練習を始めたばかりなんです。

【Yコーチ】そうですか。それでは、クイック・ターンを中心に話をしますね。まずは質問です。どういうクイック・ターンを目指していますか。

【八】勇ましく壁に突進して行き、足を高い位置から壁にぶつけるクイック・ターンが最高ですね。しぶきが大きく上がって、バッチャーンって音を聞くと、ワクワクします。

【熊】俺も同じです。どうして、壁ギリギリまで足を振り上げていられるのかなぁって思います。あれだけ力強いターンをすれば、ターンの時も、その後のスピードも、上がるのでしょうね。

【マリ】私も、ああいうダイナミックなターンが好きです。とても速そうな感じがするでしょ。只、一つ気になるのは、足を高い位置から勢いよく壁にぶつけようとするあまり、体をのけぞらしてしまうことです。壁をける時にこのフォームでは、力が出ないと思うのですが……。

【Yコーチ】皆さんのお好みのターンは同じようですね。ところで、マリさんが「のけぞる姿勢はよくないのでは？」と言われましたが、これは、当たっています。のけぞってしまうと、壁を、うまく蹴ることが出来ないし、蹴りやすい姿勢をとるには、時間をロスしてしまいます。 /370

【八】へぇー、のけぞってしまってはダメなんだ。あれ、「これは当たっている」ということは、そのほかは間違っているってことだから、俺達が理想とするターンは、良くないってことかなぁ？ /380

【Yコーチ】ええ、そうです．ところで今、三人が言われたようなクイック・ターンは、派手で恰好良く、足も速く動いているように見えますね。 /390

【八・熊・マリ】はい。 /400

【Yコーチ】スイマー自身も、達成感が高いため、速い速度で回転していると思いがちですが、これは、錯覚でしかありません。 /410

【八・熊・マリ】錯覚？ /420

【Yコーチ】えぇ、そうです。ターンは、恰好が良く、力強く見えるだけでは意味がありません。タイム的に速くなければ、良いターンとは言えないでしょう。 /430

【八・熊・マリ】それは……そうです。 /440

【Yコーチ】ターンには、「水の抵抗」の他に「角運動量保存の法則」というものが関係しています。 /450

【八・熊・マリ】角運動量保存の法則？……。 /460

【Yコーチ】はい。簡単に言えば、回転の速さは姿勢次第ということです。 /470

【熊】クイック・ターンは、姿勢が正しければ、ターンの速度も速くなるということですか。 /480

【Yコーチ】そうです。物体、例えば我々の体は、ターンする時、ターンの中心点から重さが離れている時には回りにくく、近いところに集中している時には回りやすいという性質があります。 /490

【八】「重さが離れる」って、どういう意味ですか。 /500

【Yコーチ】体の中で重い部分は、頭や足ですね。そのことを指します。ターンの時に、ターンの中心点から頭や足が遠くにあると回転しにくく、近くにあるとターンしやすくなります。頭や足が遠くに離れていると、同じ1回転をするにも、長い距離を移動することになるからです。 /510

【マリ】つまり、ターンの時には、頭や足をお腹の方に近づけて、体を、小さくしなくては、いけないのですね。 /520

【Yコーチ】えぇ、そうです。 /530

96

【八】そんなら俺、ターンの時には、早めに体を小さくするように、注意 /540
しよう。
【Yコーチ】ところが、ターンの開始時期には、体をなるべく伸ばしてお /550
いた方がいいのですよ。最初から小さくしていては、いけないのです。
【熊】それは、どうしてですか。 /560
【Yコーチ】実は、体を伸ばしている時の方が、力を出しやすいのです。 /570
ですから、体を伸ばして大きな力を与えて、それから、体を小さくして、
速く回るのがコツです。【Fig-Y（103頁）の一連の動きを見てください。】
【八】憧れのクイック・ターンが、ダメ・ターンだったとはなぁ……。 /580
【Yコーチ】残念ながらそうなんです。皆さんが先程述べたクイック・タ /590
ーンの良いところは、ターンを始めるところだけです。その後、派手に足
を壁にぶつける時に、パッチャーンの音と水しぶきが上がりますが、これ
は、力が水に吸収されたということ、つまり、力が無駄に使われていると
いうことです。こういうのを、造波抵抗とか跳水と言うのですよ。
【註：泳いでいる時に波や水しぶきを立てると悪い抵抗が発生する。】
【マリ】その言葉、本で読んだことがあります。その時は、何のことやら、 /600
さっぱり分からなかったけれど、今、少し分かりました。
【Yコーチ】それと気をつけて欲しいのは、ターンに気をとられるあまり、 /610
ターンに入る時に速度が落ちてしまうケースです。「ターンの速度は上が
った、しかし、トータルタイムは落ちた」では、シャレにもなりませんね。

～～～～～～～～～～～～～～～～～～～～～～～～～～～～～～～～

【八】今日は凄いこと教わっちゃったなぁ！　こりゃ暗記して、あのコに　　/620
聞かせなくっちゃ。熊さん、ノート、ちゃんと取ってくれただろうな。
【熊】全部、書いたけど……八つぁん、たまには、お前もやれよ、いつも　　/630
俺、ばっかり……。
【マリ】八つぁん・熊さん、コーチは仕事があるので帰ったけど、私達は、/640
もう少し飲んでからお開きにしません？
【熊】それゃ、いいなぁ。そうしよう……あれー、八つぁん、一体、何を　/650
うなっているんだい？
【八】ちょっと、黙っててくれよ、大切なトコだからな。うーん、クイッ　/660
ク・ターンでバッチャーンは……。
【熊】いい話だったじゃないか。そうだろ、八つぁん。　　　　　　　　　/670
【八】黙ってくれったら……えーと、クイック・ターンでは、「タイムか、/680
恰好か」のどちらかを選ばないと……。俺は、どっちかと言えば……。
【熊】八つぁんよ、俺は、Yコーチの話を聞いたら、バッチャーン・クイ　/690
ック・ターンが、恰好が良いとは思えなくなったぜ。
【マリ】そうよ、八つぁん。私も、考えを変えたわ。　　　　　　　　　　/700
【八】だけどなぁ、俺が、力強い男だってトコも、見せなくちゃ……。　　/710
【熊】八つぁん、今度は誰に見せたいんだい？　そうか、モモエちゃんか。/720
【八】ち、違うって……。　　　　　　　　　　　　　　　　　　　　　　/730
【マリ】八つぁん、いくらバッチャーンが好きでも、飛び込みのバッチャ　/740
ーンだけで、充分じゃないかしら……。

---- 【終り】 ----

------------------------------【参考資料】------------------------------

◆山田悟史　講演「ターンについて」中京大学水泳研究会／２００３年１０月
◆山田悟史　講演「水泳のバイオメカニクス」特定非営利活動法人スポーツ・
　ソリューション講習会／２００５年１月

[15] Don't Make A Big Splash!   /100

[Satoshi Yamada]

-------------------- (After finishing exercise) ------------------- /110
【K】 We'd better not keep him waiting for us, let's have a quick   /120
shower and go.
【H】 OK. We hear T-coach is bringing a coaching friend with him. /130
Umm, we've got a great chance!
【K】 Hat-san, Let's hurry up. Why are you looking around so   /140
restlessly?
【K】 Kuma-san, look at that guy swimming in the 4th lane! Oh!   /150
Thud!
【M】 Yippee! Somebody! Help me up.   /160
【H】 Ahh! Momoe-chan! Sorry for bumping into you. Hold my hand. /170
Oops-a-daisy! Oh, your finger looks red!
【M】 Um. I'll excuse you Hat-san. I'm all right. But please   /180
pay more attention to where you are going.
【H】 Kuma-san. Go ahead! I'd better take her to the dispensary. /190
I'll catch up later.

【K】 Momoe-chan said,"I'm all right." Oh, brother! I'm sure you /200
bumped into her on purpose. I'm spying on you. You were stepping
back and making a pretense to look at the person who was swimming,
weren't you?

【H】 Shhh! Your voice is too loud. Um, if Kuma-san were not here, /210
everything would go well…

~~~~~~

【T-coach】 Sorry for being late. Let me introduce my friend, /220
Y-coach. He also specializes in hydrodynamics.

【Y-coach】 Nice to meet you. /230

【M・H・K】 Nice to meet you, too. /240

【Y-coach】 I have heard from T-coach that the three of you are /250
very eager to study swimming techniques.

【H】 Um, I'm not so eager. But to learn... /260

【K】 Hat-san, you should be frank. Y-coach, because we feel /270
interested to hear the explanation of swimming hydrodynamics, we
will listen to your explanation eagerly.

【M】 Well, let's listen to it while we are eating. I've ordered /280
a chicken hot pot. And now, I'll order drinks……. Hey, waiter,
we'll have five schooners. What's today's theme, T-coach?

【T-coach】 As I troubled Y-coach to attend this meeting today, /290
I'd like to ask him to lecture you.

【M】 Oh! That's great! Y-coach, what do you intend to lecture /300
us about?

【Y-coach】 Well, I'm preparing to lecture about the quick turn. /310
How about that theme?

【H・K・M】 Ah, that's so nice. The three of us only began to /320
practice the free style quick turn recently.

【Y-coach】 I see. Then I'll talk about the quick turn mainly. /330
First of all I have a question to all of you. How would you
intend to do the quick turn?

【H】 After making a dash to the wall bravely, it's best that you /340
raise your legs in a high position. Then you bump your legs
against the wall at a stretch, don't you? It sounds exciting when
the spray's rising and you're making a splashing sound.

【K】 I agree with you. I wonder why you raise your legs up so /350
closely as your legs get to the wall. Doing the quick turn so
powerfully will cause the turning speed to increase after the turn
movement.

【M】I'm fond of a dynamic turn like that, too. It looks /360
very fast, doesn't it? I have something on my chest. We
seem to make an arched posture in the water, don't we?
We can't thump our legs powerfully against the wall in the
arched posture.

【Y-coach】Your favorite turn seems to be the same, doesn't it? /370
By the way Mari-san said, "the arched back posture isn't good,
is it?" It is true about this. You can't push off the wall
with the arched back posture effectively. Moreover, it takes
extra time for you to regain your posture, back to where you can
kick again easily.

【H】Oh, I got you. I understand now that the arched posture is /380
not good. Um, "It is true about this" means that the other is
wrong. Our ideal turn is not good, is it?

【Y-coach】Yes, definitely. The quick turn which the three of /390
you have now spoken about, sounds cool and moreover, seems fast
using the legs like this, doesn't it?

【M・H・K】Absolutely. /400

【Y-coach】Feeling that the effort has paid off, a swimmer has a /410
tendency to feel that their turn is ideal, but this is only an
illusion.

【M・H・K】It's an illusion? /420

【Y-coach】Oh, absolutely. It is not significant that a quick /430
turn should look cool and powerful. A good quick turn only
requires a short period of time.

【M・H・K】That is... that's right. /440

【Y-coach】A quick turn is not only related to "water drag", but /450
also to "the law of angular momentum conservation", or in other
words, the law of optimum energy use.

【M・H・K】What is "the law of angular momentum conservation"? /460

【Y-coach】Okay. Speaking briefly, the ideal turn depends on /470
your posture.

【K】The correct posture in the quick turn makes turning /480
velocity fast, doesn't it?

【Y-coach】That's right. For example, objectively our body /490
has the following properties. One, it is difficult for the
body to turn when the mass of our body pulls away from the
center of revolution, and secondly it is easy to turn when
the whole mass concentrates on a smaller point in the revolution.

【H】What does, "the mass pulls away" mean? /500

【Y-coach】The heavier parts of our body are the head and /510
legs, aren't they? That's where "the mass pulls away".
In the quick turn, it's difficult to turn when the head and
legs pull away from the center of the revolution. It's easier
to turn when the head and legs are near the center of the
revolution. When the head and legs pull away far from the
center of revolution, they move a long distance, even in the
same revolution.

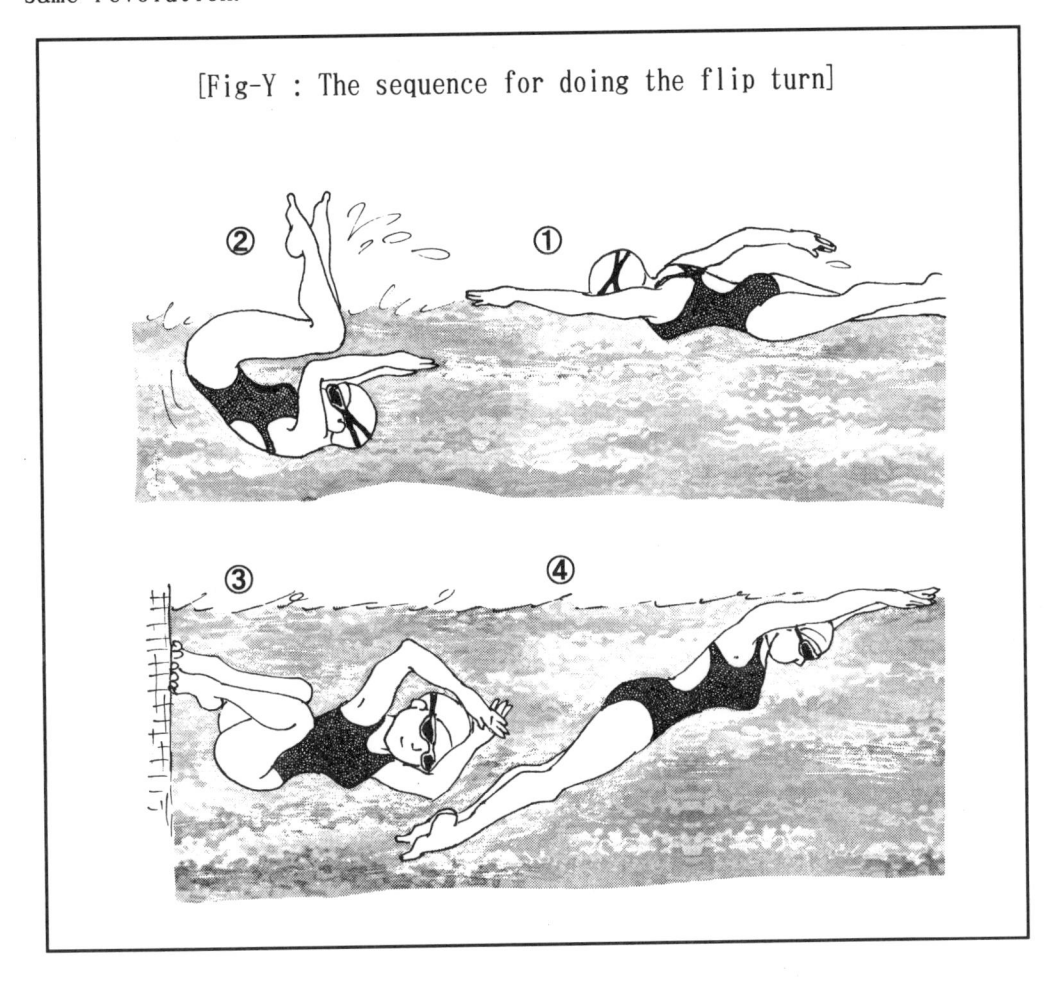

[Fig-Y : The sequence for doing the flip turn]

【M】 In other words, in the quick turn, when the head and /520
legs are brought close to the stomach, the body needs to be
smaller.

【Y-coach】 Yeah, that's right. /530

【H】 We should take care to make our body small in the quick turn /540
earlier than usual.

【Y-coach】 However, our body should be stretched out at the /550
start of the quick turn. It is no good to make our body smaller
at the beginning of the quick turn.

【K】 Why is that? /560

【Y-coach】 As a matter of fact, it is easy to conserve the body's /570
power when the posture of the body is stretched out. So, the
trick of the flip turn is that our body, when outstretched,
transfers the power for turning. Shortly afterwards, our body
which is thus made smaller, will turn quickly much more
efficiently. [See Fig-Y]

【H】 What a pity we hear that the quick turn of our dreams is /580
not useful!

【Y-coach】 It's a pity but it is true. The showy aspect you /590
mentioned a little while ago is only a small aspect of a bad
quick turn. Afterwards, when the legs are thumped into the wall
showily, the splashing sounds and the occurrence of spray, mean
that the force is absorbed by the water. That is to say, it means
that force is wastefully used. These are called, "wave drag" and
"spray drag".

[note: the wave and spray of swimming make bad drag.]

【M】 I have read those words before in a book, but at that time /600
I couldn't completely understand what was written, but now I get
the picture.

【Y-coach】 Moreover, what I expect you to pay attention to, /610
is that while being strongly conscious of the quick turn,
swimming velocity must slow down before the beginning of
the quick turn. "Turning velocity rises, but total time drops"
can't be a joke.

【H】We gained a lot of knowledge during the lecture today! /620
I have to learn it by heart. I wanna teach that girl about
it. Kuma-san, did you correctly write it down in a notebook
for us?

【K】I could perfectly write it down. Hat-san, try it for a /630
change like me.

【M】Hat-san, Kuma-san, the coaches have gone home from their /640
work. Shall we call it a day after one more drink?

【K】It's a good idea. Let's do it... Oh, Hat-san, what are you /650
groaning about?

【H】I want you not to talk to me for a moment. It's an /660
important point. Umm, the splash in the quick turn...

【K】What a nice lecture! Did you think so, Hat-san? /670

【H】Don't talk to me... Ahh, I have to choose which time or /680
figure...

【K】Hat-san, I don't think of splashing in the quick turn to be /690
so cool after receiving Y-coach's lecture.

【M】It is indeed. Hat-san, I've changed my way of thinking. /700

【H】But I dare to say. I wanna show I'm a powerful man... /710

【K】Hat-san, do you wanna show who? I've got it, it's Momoe, /720
isn't it?

【H】It's not... /730

【M】Hat-san, how fond of making a splash you are, but it may be /740
enough to be only a diving splash!

---- 【END】 ----

---------------- 【 Reference : Author's own works 】 ------------------

◆Satoshi Yamada : Lecture on "The Quick Turn of Swimming" at a Technical
   Meeting of Chukyo University. /2003 (In Japanese)

◆Satoshi Yamada : Lecture on "The Biomechanics of Swimming" at a Sport
   Solution Technical Meeting. /2005 (In Japanese)

[16] キックの流体力学

〔平木 茂子 (Shigeko Hiraki)〕

---------------- (喫茶「クロール・ストローク」にて) ----------------

【マリ】あったー！ ここよ、ここ。赤い屋根の喫茶店、あったわ！

【八】ホントだ。喫茶「クロール・ストローク」って書いてあるぞ。

【熊】名前がいいじゃないか。さぁ、中に入ろうよ。

【ウエートレス】いらっしゃいませ。三名様でしょうか。

【マリ】後から、もう一人、来ますのでお願いします。Tコーチは「仕事を済ませたらすぐ行きます」とのことだったから、お茶でも飲みながら、待ちましょうよ。それじゃ、私は、コーヒーをお願い。

【八】俺も、コーヒー。

【熊】俺は、ミルク・ティ。

【ウエートレス】かしこまりました。

【マリ】まぁー、なんてお洒落な喫茶店かしら！ 見て・見て、あすこに水泳の模様のポロシャツが置いてあるわ。ちょっと、見てくる。

【八・熊】俺達も行くよ。

【マリ】わー、素敵じゃない。背中には、クロールとか背泳とかバタフライの模様がプリントしてあって、前は、スタート台で構えている絵だわ。

【熊】いろんな色があるじゃないか。俺、1枚、買って帰ろう。

【八】プールでこんなの着て歩いたら、恰好いいなぁ。俺、絶対、買うぞ。

【マリ】八つぁん・熊さん、帰りに、ゆっくり見てから、買いましょうね。あら、Tコーチが見えたわ。

【Tコーチ】お待たせー。お腹が空いたでしょう。食事にしましょうか。

【マリ】えぇ。ここのカレーは最高だって聞いていたので、頼んでおきました。ところで、ここは、Tコーチの知り合いのお店なんですか。

【Tコーチ】大学時代の水泳部の友達がやっているんですよ。絵を描くのが大好きなヤツなんですが、親に反対されて普通の大学に入って、でも、サラリーマンが嫌で、つい最近、この店を始めたんです。

【マリ】ここの水泳グッズは、全部、そのお友達の方が作ったのですか。

【Tコーチ】はい。本当に泳いでいるみたいな絵でしょう。

【ウエートレス】お待たせー。ご注文のビーフ・カレーとサラダです。

【全員】わー、美味しそー！ いただきまーす！

～～～～～～～～～～～～～～～～～～～～～～～～～～～～～～～～～～～～～

【Tコーチ】それでは、流体力学の話、始めましょうか。　　　　　　　　/330

【ハ】Tコーチ、今日のテーマは、こちらで決めてもいいですか。　　　/340

【Tコーチ】勿論ですよ。それで、何がいいですか。　　　　　　　　　/350

【熊】さっき、三人で話し合ったのですが、今日は、キックの話をして欲　/360
しいんです。

【Tコーチ】いいですよ。でも、何でキックなんですか。　　　　　　　/370

【マリ】この前、水泳の研究会のポスターが、クラブのフロントに貼っ　/380
てあったでしょ。テーマが「クロールのキック」だったので、三人で聞き
に行ったんです。私達、三人とも、キックが悩みのタネなんで、興味があ
るんです。

【ハ】でも、研究会での話が、難しくて……。　　　　　　　　　　　/390

【熊】そうなんです。それで、俺達に研究会の内容が分かったか・どうか　/400
も、確認したいんです。

【Tコーチ】皆さん、とても研究熱心ですね。それで、研究会では、どの　/410
ような話が出たのですか。

【マリ】「理想的なクロールのキックはどうあるべきか」の話でした。　/420

【Tコーチ】具体的には？　　　　　　　　　　　　　　　　　　　　/430

【マリ】クロールでは、蹴り上げの時に足の裏で水を後方に押し出し、　/440
蹴り下げの時に足の甲で、同様に後方に水を押し出し、その反作用で推進
力を得ているとの説明でした。

【ハ】最後に講師の方が、このようなキックをすれば、キックの力が効率　/450
よく推進力に変わるのでムダがないから、このキックを目指すようにと、
言われました。

【Tコーチ】皆さん、よくそこまで理解したと思いますが、その説明は、　/460
正しくないと思います。

【全員】えっ、正しくないって？　　　　　　　　　　　　　　　　　/470

【Tコーチ】はい。クロールのキックの推進力は、足の甲や足の裏で水を　/480
後方に押し出して得ているのではありません。

【マリ】でも、私、前に流体力学の本を読んだ時にも、そのようなことが　/490
書いてあったと記憶していますが……。

【Tコーチ】多分、その頃の流体力学では、それが、精一杯の分析だった　/500
のではないでしょうか。

【マリ】そうでしたか……。　　　　　　　　　　　　　　　　　　　/510

【Tコーチ】クロールのキックのメカニズムは、誤解しがちなので、詳しく説明します。まず、足の甲や足の裏を後方に動かす速度は、泳ぐ速さより遅いという事実があります。もっと詳しく言うと、泳いでいる時に、スイマーには、泳ぐ速度に応じて、前から水が流れて来ます。速く泳げば泳ぐほど、スイマーには前方から水が速く流れて来ます。もし、この水の速さより速く、足の甲や足の裏を後方に動かすことが出来れば、キックによる推進力が発生すると思いますが、それは人間には不可能です。 /520

【マリ・八・熊】ほぅ……。 /530

【Tコーチ】実験データを解析した結果を見ても、スイマーがいかに速く泳ごうとも、水の速さよりも速く、足の甲や足の裏を後方に動かしてはいません。従って、このようなキック〔足の甲や足の裏を使うキック〕を使えば、マイナスの推力が発生します。 /540

【マリ】それでは、クロールのキックは、どうすればいいのですか。 /550

【Tコーチ】クロールでは、足のつま先を上下に動かすだけで、キックの推進力が発生します。 /560

【熊】どうして、つま先を上下に動かすだけでいいのですか。 /570

【Tコーチ】実際の動作ではありませんが、つま先を上下に動かしたとしても、後方に一対の渦が発生し、その渦により、後方に向かってジェット水流が発生します。このジェット水流の反作用でキックの推進力が生まれます。 /580

【熊】Tコーチ、ノートにきちんと整理しておきたいので、クロールのキックの注意事項、もう一度、お願いします。 /590

【Tコーチ】はい。クロールのキックでは、膝を大きく曲げると、抵抗が大きくなります。しかし、膝を曲げないとキックは出来ません。ですから、上下動が出来る程度に膝を曲げて、キックをしてください。 /600

【八】そのキックは、先程の、「つま先を上下に動かすキック」ですね。 /610

【Tコーチ】そうです。 /620

【マリ・八・熊】今日は、びっくりすることばっかりで……。 /630

流体力学ではこういう上下のキック

【Tコーチ】私自身も、以前は、皆さんが研究会で聞いた説明の通りだと　　/640
思っていました。しかし、ある時期から、おかしいと思って、ずーっと、
研究を続けてきました。

【マリ】Tコーチは、アメリカやニュージーランドやその他の国の学会で、/650
何度も発表されたそうですが、それが、この理論なんですね。

【Tコーチ】えぇ、そうです。発表の後では、質問が殺到して大変でした。/660
クロールのキックも推力や抵抗を計算できることを世界に示せて、良かっ
たと思いました。

～～～～～～～～～～～～～～～～～～～～～～～～～～～～～～

【マリ】八つぁんと熊さんは、何色のポロシャツにする？　私は、背泳の　/670
模様が入っている黄色のに決めるわ。

【八】俺、クロールの絵のピンクがいいや。　　　　　　　　　　　　　/680

【熊】俺は、平泳ぎが描いてある黒にするか。　　　　　　　　　　　　/690

【八】熊さんが黒を着たら、本物の熊だぜ。別の色にしろよ。　　　　　/700

【熊】そうか、それじゃ、白でいくか。　　　　　　　　　　　　　　　/710

【マリ】それだと、白熊だわ。　　　　　　　　　　　　　　　　　　　/720

【熊】うーん、そんなら、赤にするか。　　　　　　　　　　　　　　　/730

【マリ】熊さん、赤なら、緋・熊〔ひぐま〕、赤熊になっちゃうわ！　　/740

---- 【終り】 ----

------------------------------【参考資料】------------------------------

◆竹島良憲・高橋繁浩・山田悟史
　「クロールキックの抗力推力（Pressure Drop Thrust）は利用可能か」日本体育
　　学会第54回大会（バイオメカニクス）／2003年　於：熊本市・熊本大学

◆竹島良憲・高橋繁浩・山田悟史
　「クロールキックの推力計算」「Culculation of front crawl stroke kick
　　thrust」第19回国際バイオメカニクス学会／2003年　於：ニュージーラ
　　ンド・ダニーデン市・オタゴ大学

◆竹島良憲・高橋繁浩・山田悟史
　「クロールキックの抵抗計算」「Calculation of front crawl stroke kick drag」
　　第5回国際スポーツエンジニアリング学会／2004年　於：米国・カルフォ
　　ルニア州・ディヴィス市・カルフォルニア大学

[16] Hydrodynamics Of Kicking /100

[Yoshinori Takeshima]

----------------(In the cafeteria,"Crawl Stroke") ---------------- /110

【M】 We've found it! Here we are. The red roofed cafeteria. /120
We've done it!

【H】 You're absolutely right. Can you see the cafeteria named /130
"Crawl Stroke".

【K】 I like the name. Let's go inside. /140

【Waitress】 May I help you? Is there three of you? /150

【M】 Later another will come. T-coach said, "I'll go as soon as /160
I can after work". Let's have something to drink to kill some
time until he comes. I'll have a cup of coffee.

【H】 Coffee for me also. /170

【K】 I'll have a milk tea. /180

【Waitress】 Yes, sir. /190

【M】 How fashionable this cafeteria is! Look!, look! Can you /200
see that polo shirt with a swimming pattern on it over there.
I'll go and have a look at it.

【H・M】We'll go, too. /210

【M】Woo! How cool it is! It's printed with crawl stroke, Back /220
stroke and Butterfly on the back and Standing start on the front.

【K】There are several colors, aren't there? I'll buy a shirt. /230

【H】It's cool for you to walk around wearing a shirt like this /240
one by the pool. I'll absolutely buy something.

【M】Hat-san, Kuma-san, we will have enough time to look at them /250
after our meeting. How about buying something after we have our
meeting?

【T-coach】I'm sorry to have kept you waiting. /260
You look like your hungry. Let's have a meal.

【M】Yes. Since I have heard this cafeteria serves great curry, /270
I have already ordered it for us. By the way T-coach, have you
and the master of this shop known each other for all of your lives?

【T-coach】My friend runs the business here. He and I were in /280
a swimming club during college days. He's very fond of painting.
He was eager to apply for admittance to an art college, but he
entered a normal college in spite of his parents.
His patience was worn out as an office worker, so he started to
run this business only recently.

【M】Did your friend make all these swimming goods? /290

【T-coach】Absolutely. You think his paintings are very /300
realistic, don't you?

【Waitress】Here are your meals. Beef curries and salads. /310

【A】Wow! It looks so delicious. Good appetite! /320

【T-coach】Well, let's begin the explanation on hydrodynamics. /330

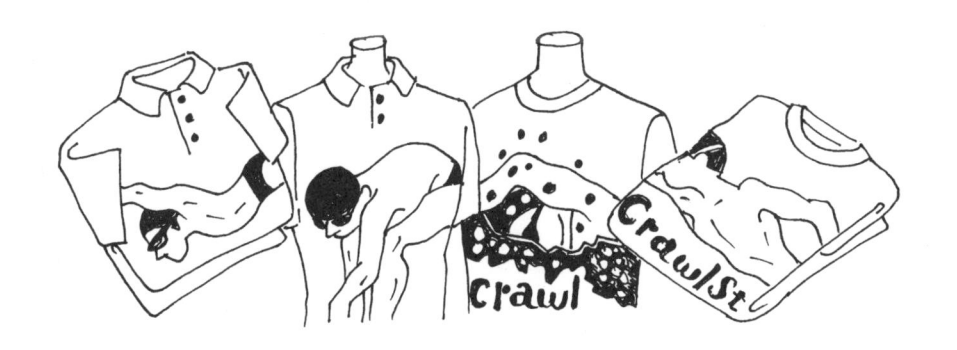

【H】 T-coach, may we propose today's theme? /340

【T-coach】 Of course! Sure! What shall I talk about? /350

【K】 The three of us have spoken about it together and we want /360
you to lecture us on kicking.

【T-coach】 All right, but I wonder why it is to be about kicking? /370

【M】 Recently, we saw a poster on a swimming lecture posted by /380
the club reception desk. The three of us participated in the
lecture because of it's theme on the crawl stroke kick. Since we
are not good at kicking, we are interested in it.

【H】 But, the lecture content is so difficult... /390

【K】 That's right. We want to check with you if we can /400
understand correctly the content of that lecture.

【T-coach】 You are all eager to study, aren't you? What did you /410
study at the lecture?

【M】 Its content was about how to kick perfectly while doing /420
the crawl stroke.

【T-coach】 Will you elaborate on it? /430

【M】 It is explained that in the crawl stroke, a swimmer pushes /440
water backward by the sole of the foot in the up kick and by the
step of the foot in the down kick. Thus, he can obtain a thrust
reaction by pushing water backwards.

【H】 Because the force of the kick is turned into thrust /450
efficiently by this technique, we should aim at doing this
in this way.

【T-coach】 So you get it to some extent but the explanation /460
is not quite correct.

【M・H・K】 It is not correct, is it? /470

【T-coach】 No, it's not correct that you gain kick thrust to push /480
water backward by the instep and shin, or sole and calf.

【M】 But, I remember that I read it written in the book of /490
hydrodynamics?...

【T-coach】 Maybe the study of swimming analysis in those days /500
was very limited concerning hydrodynamics.

【M】Is that right? /510

【T-coach】Since you are likely to mistake the process of the /520
kicking in the crawl stroke, I'll explain it in detail.
First you have the fact that the velocity of the instep and shin,
which are moving backward, is slower than the swimming velocity.
I'll give you a specific account of it. When you swim, water
flows from the front according to your swimming velocity, as shown
in Fig-T (upper). If you can move your instep or shin backward
faster than the flowing velocity from the front, you are able to
obtain the thrust by moving your instep or shin backward.
It is impossible for human beings.

【M・H・K】It is indeed. /530

【T-coach】You will find that a swimmer can't move his instep and /540
shin backwards faster than his swimming velocity to see the result
of swimming experiment datum. If you swim using this kicking, that
is to say, using the shin and sole of the foot, minus thrust occurs.

【M】According to your kick theory, will you teach us how to /550
kick properly in the crawl stroke?

【T-coach】In crawl stroke, kicking thrust occurs by moving the /560
tiptoes up and down.

【K】Is it enough only to move the tiptoes up and down? /570

【T-coach】A pair of vortexes occur to the rear of the foot even /580
when only moving the tiptoes up and down. A jet stream occurs
flowing backward as shown in Fig-T (lower). The kicking thrust
develops on account of reaction to this jet stream.

【K】I'd like to write down what you have taught us. Would you /590
talk about it again?

【T-coach】The style of the crawl stroke creates drag as well as /600
thrust. So, the bigger you bend your knee, the more drag occurs.
But you can't kick without bending your knee. So you should
bend your knee to some extent that you can move up and down to
prevent drag, and then, increase thrust.

【H】So, your previous explanation about "Kicking by moving your /610
tiptoes up and down", will improve our kicking?

【 Fig-T : The mechanics of kicking 】

【This kicking style is considered as bad】

① The speed of the instep moving backwards in the down kick = V

② The speed of the sole moving backwards in the up kick = V

③ The flow speed from the front is equal to the swimming speed = U

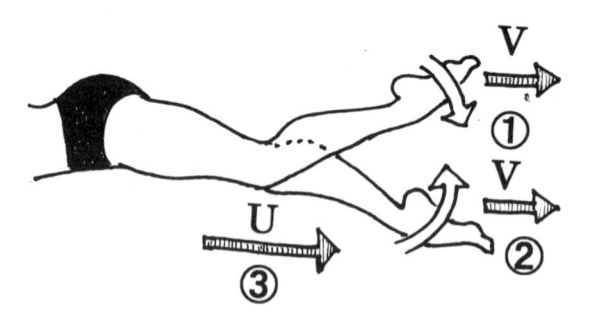

If U > V, minus thrust occurs.

【The ideal kick according to hydrodynamics】

④ A vortex occurs in the up kick

⑤ A vortex occurs in the down kick

⑥ A jet stream occurs due to the pair of vortexes rotating inversely

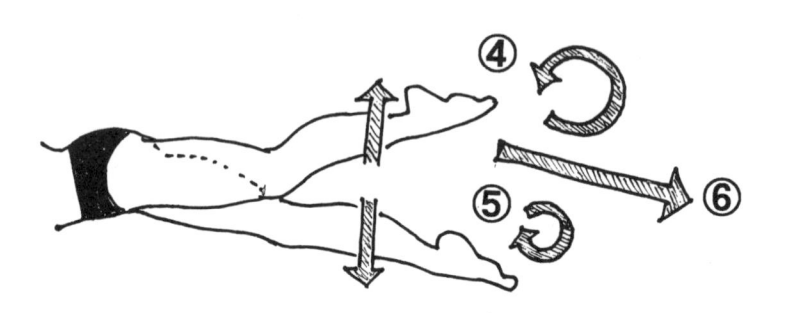

【T-coach】That's right. /620

【M・H・K】We are very surprised by what we have heard today... /630

【T-coach】For myself, I used to believe the same as what you /640
have heard at the workshops you have been to. At times, I doubted
the theory of kick thrust and I have continued to research
improvements to the theory.

【M】 We heard that T-coach presented this research several times /650
at the international congress. It is the topic of today's lecture,
isn't it?

【T-coach】 Yes. I was embarrassed to be asked so many questions /660
after my presentation. I would think that it is my pleasure to
have shown to the swimming world circle of various countries that
we can even calculate the thrust and drag of the kicking in the
crawl stroke.

~~~~~~

【M】 Hat-san, Kuma-san, what color poloshirt do you prefer? /670
For myself, I've decided on this one which has the printed
back stroke on it.

【H】 I like the pink printing which has the crawl stroke. /680

【K】 I'm fond of the black one, which has the printed breast /690
stroke on it.

【H】 Kuma-san, you seem like the true bear if you wear the black /700
poloshirt. You should choose another color.

【K】 Perhaps you are right. I'll choose the white one. /710

【M】 That means white bear. /720

【K】 Wait on! Is the brown one OK? /730

【M】 If Kuma-san wears the brown one, you become the brown bear! /740

---- 【END】 ----

------------------ 【 Reference : Author's own works 】 ------------------

◆Yoshinori Takeshima ・ Shigehiro Takahashi・ Satoshi Yamada
「Utilization to Pressure Drop Thrust in front crawl stroke kick」 In the
Proceeding of Japanese Society of Physical Education Health Sport Science
54th annual meeting /2003 : Kumamoto University, Kumamoto,

◆Yoshinori Takeshima ・ Shigehiro Takahashi・ Satoshi Yamada
「Culculation of front crawl stroke kick thrust」 In the Proceedings of
19th ISB/2003 : Otago University, Dunedin, New Zealand.

◆Yoshinori Takeshima ・ Shigehiro Takahashi・ Satoshi Yamada
「Calculation of front crawl stroke kick drag」 In the Proceedings of 5th
ISEA/2004 : California University, Davis, USA.

IV. 楽しくなったらここを読もう！

[1] 落語豆知識

　　　　　　　　　　　　　　　　　　　　今井　恒雄（Tsuneo Imai）

　落語は演芸のひとつで、滑稽な話をし、その最後にオチをつけて私達を楽しませてくれます。江戸時代の末期から明治時代にかけて成熟したので、その時代の風俗を背景にした話が中心になっています。

　落語の生命は笑いです。笑いにも、人の欠点・失敗を笑う程度の低いものから、暖かい人情味溢れた高度なユーモアまで色々ありますが、優れた落語は、優れたユーモアに裏付けされています。

　ほんの一言で話に結末をつけ、盛り上げるオチは、話そのものと同じぐらい重要な要素です。落語は普通３つの部分で構成されます。「マクラ・本題・オチ」の３つです。これについて簡単に解説しましょう。

1.　マクラ：本題に入る前の導入部を「マクラ」といいます。多くは、世間話とか気のきいた小ばなしをします。世間話は、天気のことでも、身辺の出来事でもなんでもよくて、ただ、軽いユーモアでお客の気分をほぐし、うまく本題につなぐようなものにします。

2.　本題：落語は本質的に会話で成り立っています。情景や心理を描写するのにも、出来るだけ説明に頼らず、登場人物のセリフと仕種で表現するのが特長です。つまり落語は耳から聞くだけの芸ではなく、目で見て楽しむ芸でもあります。言葉での説明と会話で描写の違いを見てみましょう。

　　「口で説明」　拾い上げたのは、ずっしりと重い財布。中をみますと、確かに
　　　　　　　　　金。びっくりして財布をまるめ懐にねじこむ。
　　「落語」　　　（財布を拾う仕草）「おっそろしく汚ねえ財布だなぁ。」
　　　　　　　　　（と、中身をみて少しずつ体が震え出しし財布を丸めて懐にねじこむ仕草）

3.　オチ：機知に富んだ話の結末のことを指します。オチは落語の生命ですから、練りに練って作られ、また様々な形があります。いずれにしてもオチの演出には、凝縮度・集中度の高さが求められるのです。

　ここで、落語《禁酒》を例にして、本題とオチ関係の例をみましょう。マクラは省略、本題は要約してあります。

------------- 《禁酒》-------------

「本題」「おい、一杯飲まねえか。」
　　　　「駄目だ、神様に願掛けして、向こう一年禁酒したんだ。」
　　　　「つまらねえことをしやがったなぁ、朝昼晩飲んでた奴が、急に飲まなくなると、かえって体によくねえぞ。どうだい、一年を二年に延ばして、晩酌だけやらしてもらったら？」
　　　　「そうだなぁ、そういう手があったか……。」
「オチ」「じゃァ、いっそのこと三年にして、朝晩飲もう。」

　この最後の一言を、絶妙の間（ま）と言い回しでさらりとやるところに、オチの神髄があります。

~~~~~~~~~~~~~~~~~~~~~~~~~~~~~~~~~~~~~~

　私達の話には、八つぁんと熊さんが、主人公として登場します。この二人は、昔から落語に登場して来ました。二人とも貧乏で、お人好しの正直者です。教育は殆ど受けていません。仕事は職人の手伝いとか使い走りなどです。この二人の名前とキャラクタを使ったのは、彼らの口を借りて、次のようなことを言いたかったからです。◆勉強はいくつになっても始められる。◆一歩を踏み出す勇気を持とう！◆繰り返すことが出来れば成功する等々。コンピュータの世界（前著）、水泳の世界、落語の世界での、ホントの話を書きました。

IV. Let's Read This Section If You Find Rakugo Interesting

[1] What Is RAKUGO?

Tsuneo Imai

RAKUGO is one of the traditional Japanese entertainments. It is made up of funny talk and a punch line. We appreciate RAKUGO very much. RAKUGO flowered at the end of the Edo period and the start of the Meiji period. So that the background of the story draws from customs and practices at that time.

Laughter is everything to RAKUGO. There are many kinds of laughter. For example, a low level one that laughs at one's failure or one's flaw in character, and a high level one that is full of humor that is warm and hearty. A great work of RAKUGO is supported with excellent humor.

The punch line is important as well as the main story, because it not only is an ending, but also it arouses the story. RAKUGO is made up of three sections. They are the introduction, subject and punch line.

Now, I will simply introduce you to these sections.

1. Introduction : An entry section of RAKUGO called "MAKURA".
Many comic storytellers talk about gossip or funny short stories. Gossip will be the happenings of the day. The important point is to darw tension from the audience and link it to the main subject of the story.

2. Subject : RAKUGO consists essentially of conversation. When comic storytellers create a picture of a scene or of the heart, they describe a story by using speech and gestures. They try as much as possible not to use explanations. We understand that RAKUGO is a performance not only to listen with one's ears, but also to watch with one's eyes.

I will show you the difference between an explanation with words and a description by conversation.

★ Explanation with words : He picked up a very heavy wallet and when he looked inside it, he found money beyond question. He was surprised and twisted it into his pocket.

★ RAKUGO : (gesture of picking up a wallet)「It's quite a dirty wallet」(And, the next gesture is twisting it into his pocket while quivering about how much money he has found in it.)

★ Punch line : A punch line is a witty ending to the story. The punch line is very important for RAKUGO. So, they polish it up, again and again. There are many styles of punch lines. Anyway, the telling of the punch line demands a high level of technique.

Now, I will show you an example of relation between subject and punch line, using a famous classic RAKUGO named "Stop Drinking Sake". I have skiped "MAKURA" and summarized the subject.

------------- 《Stop Driking Sake》 -------------

[Subject] 「Hi, let's drink sake!」「No. I prayed to God and I vowed to stop drinking for a year from now.」「It's stupid of you to stop drinking because it was habitual for you to drink every morning, afternoon and evening. So, It's not good for your health to give up completely. How about the idea that you'll drink sake only in the evening for the next two years instead.」「Yes, it's a good idea...」

[Punch line]「OK! I'll change it to three years and drink sake every morning and evening as well.」

The essence of the punch line is to speak with exuisite timing and expression.

~~~~~~

In our rakugo stories, the main characters are Hat-san and Kuma-san. These two guys' names were appeared since old time in rakugo. Both are very poor, innocent, honest and non-educated nearby. Their job is a helper for workman or an errand.

We use their names and the characters because we want to say something using Hat-san and Kuma-san's conversation as follows;

◆Anyone could start studying at anytime and at any age.
◆Let's have guts to take a step forward.
◆The key for success is repeating the practice and so on.

We wrote the real stories about computer world (in the previous book), swimming world and rakugo world.

[2] ENGLISH RAKUGO

山本 正昭 (Yamamoto Masaaki)

1. 落語とは

　英語落語を演じる前に、落語の素晴らしさについて考えてみたいと思います。「たかが落語、されど落語。」と言う表現があるように非常に奥が深く、また世界にはストーリーテラーなるプロも多く存在しますが、それと比べこれ程までユニークで芸の深いものは存在しないと思います。

　① 正座をする事によってのみ出来る。

　② 他国のストーリーテリングは話し手のキャラクターを投じ、どれだけ声のものまねが出来るかが重要ですが、落語の場合演じる人物個人のキャラクターが大いに影響します。どちらかと言うと落語は、声は演者自身の声になります。

　これら二つが大きな特徴です。その他、色々なテクニックがありますが、これは後で説明します。「落語は世界に類をみないユニークな話芸である。」これをまず頭に入れて下さい。

2. 英語落語の誕生

　英語落語が誕生したのは1983年に爆笑王と言われた桂枝雀さんが、私の英会話学校ＨＯＥインターナショナルに英会話を習いに来られたことからはじまります。枝雀さんは語学が好きで、他の英会話学校に行っては月謝だけを納め長続きしませんでした。

しかし私との出会いにより、「英会話の勉強は言葉に情をどれだけ入れるかによる。」等の話に意気投合し、私の学校には殆ど休まず、お亡くなりになるまで通われました。枝雀さんの偉い所は一度それを認めると、私のような人物にでも従って熱心に勉強される事でした。まずはアクションを使っての訓練。それからIMPROVISATION（寸劇）とリスニングの訓練。枝雀さんは神戸大学に入学される程の頭脳の持ち主、マスターも早かったです。しかし我々の年代はすぐに文法の事が気になり、なかなか流暢に話すのは難しいです。そしていざ外国人とのフリートーキングの段階に入り、若くて美人のアメリカ人女性、アン・グラブさんと二人きりになりました。しかしあまり会話が弾みません。「枝雀さん、心から何か話したい事はありませんか。」私の質問に「それは落語しかおまへん。」「では落語を翻訳してみようではありませんか。」そして英語落語の第一歩が始まるのです。

3. 英語落語は国際交流に貢献

枝雀さん、アンさんと私三人で短い笑い話ＳＲ(Short Rakugo)と名づけ、２０作ほど完成。そして古典落語「夏の医者」"Summer Doctor"に挑戦しました。

しかしこのアメリカ人女性アンさんが帰国。その後しばらくして「枝雀さん、アンさんの家に遊びに行きませんか。」と私の誘いに私達はアメリカに行く事になりました。ニューヨークからレンタカーを借り、ペンシルバニア、スクラントンの近くまでドライブし、着いたところは村中全員名前を知っているような小さな村でした。そしてアンさんの家に泊めてもらい、子供のようにはしゃぎ、遊びまわった記憶は今でも鮮明に覚えています。

アンさんは突然「枝雀さん、村の人達にあの翻訳した落語を披露してみましょうよ。」と提案。しかし小さな村にはホールもなく、野原にマットを積み上げ、即席に山台を作りトラクターのライトが照明になり、村中の人が５０人近く集まりました。その頃の彼らの持つ日本人のイメージはエコノミックアニマルでジョークのセンスもないと言った感じで、奇妙なものを見るように私達を遠巻きに見ていました。その証拠に、誰も私達に近づこうとしません。私達の落語の前に、村の若い衆５〜６人がギターと手話のコーラスを披露し、終わると同時に大きな拍手。次は私達の番です。私は少し緊張しながら舞台（？）に立ち"Ladies and Gentleman. Let me introduce you a famous storyteller in Japan, Katsura Shijaku. Please give him a big hand."　当然拍手はまばら、無理もありません。日本では、爆笑王とまで言われていた枝雀さんですが、彼らにとっては風変わりな日本人として写っていたのですから。

かくして初の英語落語海外公演は幕を上げました。やはり芸の力は凄いですね。最初はあまり興味を示さなかった村人達も、だんだんこの話に引き込まれて行くのが誰の目にもはっきり分かり、そして終わるや否や全員が枝雀さんの周りに駆け寄り、握手はもちろんの事、サイン、キスをしてくる人までそれはエキサイティングな瞬間でした。それだけではなく、驚いた事に次の日から私にまで違った態度で本当に親しげに近寄り、「今まで日本人を誤解していた。悪かった、我々と同じ人間だな。」と言いたげです。その後本当に村の人達と打ち解け、この旅を楽しむ事が出来ました。「そうだ、この英語落語を世界に広めれば国際交流に貢献できるのでは……。」

　落語は人間の基本を表現したもので、イデオロギー、政治、流行とは関係ないもので、どの国の人達にも共通の話題で構成されています。海外公演の時、私はMC担当でお気に入りのフレーズを紹介します。"All Rakugo stories tell about daily experience of Japanese people in humorous, and light hearted way. They invite the audience to share and laugh at vanities, fears, hopes and weaknesses that are familiar to all people. When we are hungry, we eat, when we are sad, we cry. All people in the world are the same."です。基本的には皆同じ心や考え方を持っていると言う事を知れば戦争など無くなるのでは……。「これを世界に広めるのだ！」枝雀さんも、口では「そんな大それた事は考えていません。」とおっしゃっていましたが、心では同意していたのが分かりました。

　まず日本に帰国してHOE主催「第１回桂枝雀英語落語独演会」を、テイジンホールにて催しました。（１９８５年７月）落語を英語で！今だかつてない公演会！テレビ、ラジオなどで取り上げられ、大センセーションを巻き起こし、翌月追加公演をせざる得なくなりました。以来朝日生命ホール等で１２回、サンケイホールで１０回と年２回定期公演が続きました。しかし１９９９年４月、枝雀さんがお亡くなりになり、本当にこれから世界に広めようと張り切っていただけに、非常に残念です。偉大な枝雀さんだったからこそ、意味があったのです。それは英語がいくら流暢に話せても、落語が上手くないと英語落語の良さを理解してもらえないからです。枝雀さんと私はアメリカ、カナダ、オーストラリア、イギリス等、主要都市３０ヶ所以上公演しました。そして毎回、私もMCとThis is Rakugo で枝雀さんと共演させて頂きました。今となっては、沢山枝雀さんとの思い出があり、色々な事を枝雀さんから学びました。

　その後も定期公演は続き、ビル・クラウリー、桂かい枝、ダイアン・吉日、桂あさ吉、林家染太などプロで活躍する演者も出てきました。

私の教室では「英語落語道場」を開講し、多くの人が英語落語を学んでいます。また、国際交流団体や高校・大学等にも「英語落語出前」と称し、演者を派遣し全国で公演を続けています。私の夢は「全国英語落語コンテスト」否「世界英語落語コンテスト」を催し、いつか柔道のように世界に広める事です。

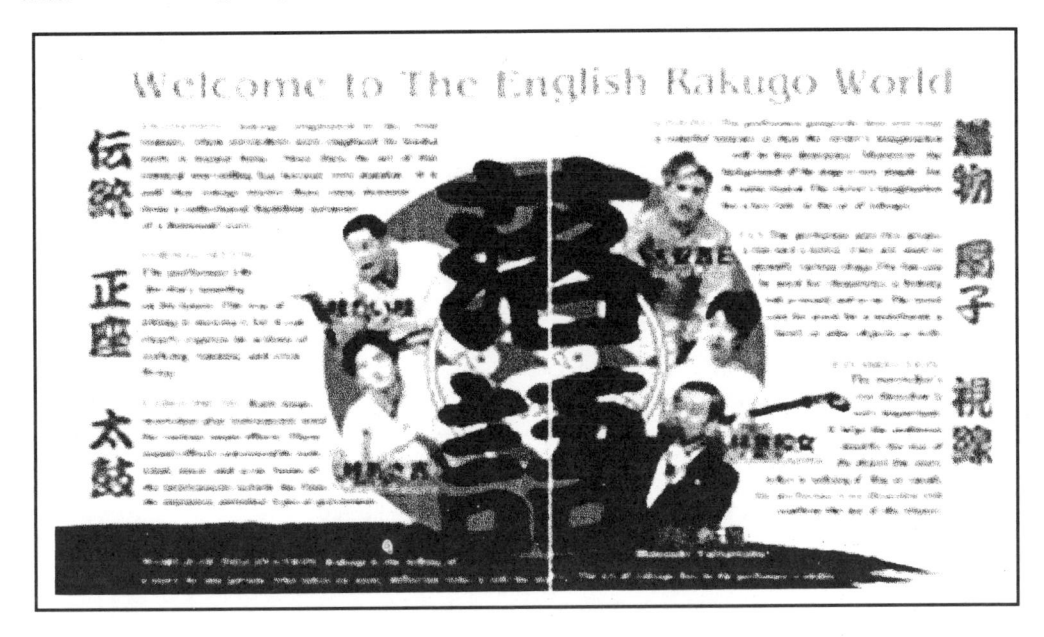

2001年　ＨＯＥロンドン公演より

4.　英語落語は英語の勉強に最適

　私は世紀の大発見をしました。少しオーバーですね。実は「落語」と「漫才」の違いを発見したのです。皆さんはお分かりですか。もちろん"一人と二人"ではありません。ではヒントを差し上げます。落語にはテープ、ＣＤそしてビデオまでありますが、漫才には殆どありません。どちらも聞いていておもしろいので、漫才にビデオなどがあってもおかしくないですね。不思議ですね。実は漫才はギャグで構成されています。皆さんはこんなギャグを知っていますか。「悪の十字架」とか「恐怖の味噌汁」。これは「開くの10時か」と「今日ふの味噌汁」です。全国的に流行りましたが、すぐに廃れましたね。なぜならギャグは、1回目はおもしろのですが、2回目はそれ程おもしろくありません。3回目ともなれば全然おもしろくなくなります。漫才もこれと同じで1回目はおもしろのですが、2回目はあまりおもしろくないので、皆さんも同じ漫才を聞いた事がないと思います。しかし赤ちゃんを見れば可愛いですね。2回目は可愛くないですか。そんな事はないですね。つまり人間の情はリピテーションが出来るのです。落語はこの情が中心なのです。それで落語は繰り返し聞く事が出来るのです。落語は「情」漫才は「知」になるのです。

人間の脳は右脳、左脳に分かれています。左脳が「知」、右脳が「情」なのです。今まで日本人が英語を勉強して来た方法では、この左脳を中心に頭で翻訳し文法を考えていたので、英語を感じていませんでした。しかし皆さんが"Thank you." "Good bye." "I love you."などの文章は訳さずに感じていますね。全ての文章を感じる事が出来れば、英語をマスターする事が出来ます。まさにこれは"Feel in English."なのです。例えばゲジゲジが歩く時、右の三つ目の足を動かして、次は左の四つ目を動かして等、考えていては歩けません。言葉も同様で感じた事を無意識に言葉に出さなくてはなりません。それにはどうすれば良いかと言えば、アクションで覚える事です。あなたが友人に車で自分の家までの道順を教えるとします。あなたが運転して、友人を助手席に乗せて教えても容易には覚える事が出来ません。しかし友人に運転させあなたが助手席で指示すれば、簡単に道を覚える事が出来るのです。同じように、英語を学ぶ時、Please pick up a pen. と言われればアクションを伴ってペンを拾う動作をすれば良いのです。

　中学校１年で文法など教えず"Please stand up. Go to the window. Open it. Come back. Sit down. Pick up a pen. Write your name on the paper..." 等々毎日命令文で動作をすれば、自然と英語を感じる事ができます。その次にIMPROVISATION（寸劇）をするのです。３年になって落語を覚え言葉に気持ちを入れる練習をすればブロークンながら会話が出来るようになります。ここから文法を学べばいいのです。皆さんは赤ちゃんの頃、お母さんから日本語の文法「かろ、かつ、く、い、い、けれ」「だろ、だっ」……等を教えてもらった記憶がありますか。日本語会話がペラペラになってから文法を学びましたね。最近ではそれ程でもありませんが、私が学生の頃は英語の先生でも英会話が出来ませんでした。そして学生がスラスラと英語の本を読んでいるのですが、内容までは理解出来ていないようです。それは、＠？＃、％＆＠と言っているのと同じでまるで暗号を読んでいるのと同じで、まるで暗号を読んでいるようなのです。そして読み終えてから翻訳するのです。日本人は中学校３年、高校３年、大学４年と合計１０年も英語の勉強をしていても話せないのは「世界七不思議の中の一つ」と言われても仕方がありません。ではこの情を入れて話す落語にチャレンジして見ましょう。その前に落語の演じ方を簡単に解説しましょう。

5.　How to perform English Rakugo（演じ方の基本）
　落語には色々な約束事がありますが、ここでは最低限度覚えておかなければならない事を述べておきます。

By changing the direction of your face, you can perform as if two people are talking.

　顔を左右に振り分ける事によって、複数の人物を演じる事が出来ます。この場合、上（かみ）下（しも）があり、偉い人は右を向いて話し、目下もしくは訪問者は左を向いて話します。

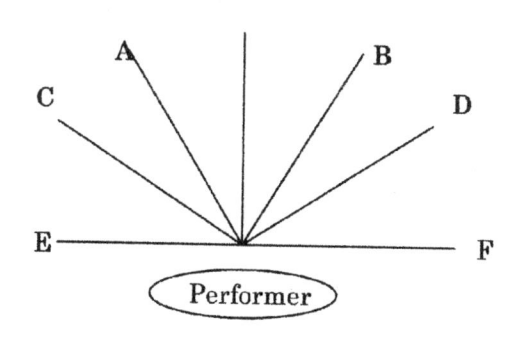

　Aに話しかけた後、答えるのはBの方向。CにしかけるとDの方向で答えます。Eの場合はFになります。

The performer uses two props, a fan and a towel.

　演者は扇子とタオルを使います。扇子は箸、棒、ペン等になり、タオルは財布、手紙、やきいも等になります。イマジネーションの世界に引き込むには、よりリアルなパントマイムが効果を高めます。

タオルが本になる。扇子が箸になる。

Pauses, intonation and facial expressions are the most important elements for Rakugo.

　間（ま）は落語では一番大切な事と言われています。あまり練習しすぎて覚えた文をスラスラと話すのは、聞き手にとって話しについて行けない場合があります。特に英語落語の場合、文と文の間に間（ま）を持つ必要があります。何故ならば、その間に聞き手は英語の意味を理解出来るからです。また少し休憩にもなります。もちろん演者は言葉に感情を注入し、顔の表情を加え抑揚を付けて話さなければなりません。

Eye direction describes the size big and small and also movements.

目線で物の大きさ、長さ等を観客に想像させます。また物の動き、早さ等も表現する事が出来ます。二人の人物を想像させるにはしっかりと同じ位置に目線を定めなければなりません。もちろん目で喜び、驚き、恐怖を表す事も出来ます。

目線を定める

目線で大きさを表現

目線で動きを表現

目線で長さを表現

目線の速さでスピードを表す

目線で長さを表現

Every Rakugo ends with a punch line.
　落語は読んで字のごとく落とし話です。オチは下げとも言われています。このオチの為に話を仕込んでおきます。そして最後に少し間を持って大きめの声でオチの言葉を発します。

Stage height: Audience should be able to see the performer's knees.
　演者の座っている台を山台と言います。演者は意外と高い位置となります。理想的なのは、後ろの席からでも演者の膝が見える位の高さが必要です。

Sound effects, which we call Ohayashi: The music players are on side of the stage, not only playing music but also makes sound of snow, rain and so on.
　舞台の袖にお囃子と呼ばれる三味線、太鼓、笛などを演奏する者がいます。客席からは見る事は出来ませんが、演奏者は演者の噺に合わせて曲や効果音を奏でます。また、開演30分前に一番太鼓「ドンと来い、ドンと来い。」と聞こえる音を出し、開演寸前に二番太鼓、そして出囃子を演奏します。これは演者が好きな曲を選ぶ事が出来ます。演者が席に着くと曲をストップさせます。そして噺がスタートし、そしてオチを言ったと同時に太鼓で「ドンドン」と叩き、入り囃子が鳴ります。その後演者が退場します。また公演の終わりには「追い出し太鼓」を叩きます。

The music players use these instruments below.
　お囃子で使用する楽器は次頁の図に示したものです。

三味線	笛	大太鼓

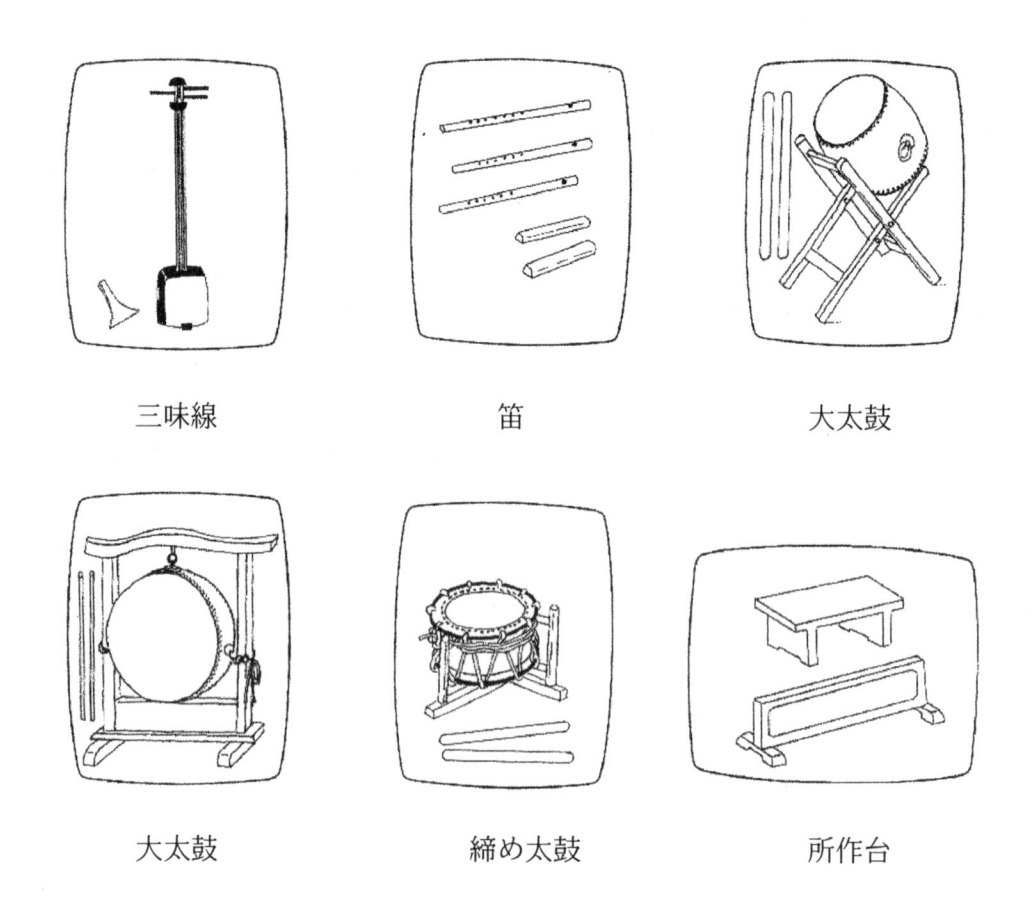

大太鼓	締め太鼓	所作台

Ochako: Usually, an assistant lady turns cushion on stage, and turns the Mekuri, which shows the performers name and the title of the performance on the long paper, at the beginning of each performance.

お茶子は女性アシスタントで、山台にある座布団をひっくり返して名びら台の名びらをめくる役目をします。演者の脱いだ羽織を持って退場したり、また所作台を引っ込めたりします。

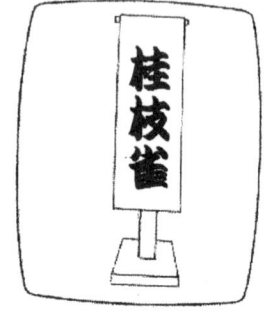

I hope you could understand the Rakugo much better than before. When you perform English Rakugo, please use your imagination.

英語落語について少しはお分かりになったと思います。一度自分でこの英語落語を演じてみて下さい。きっとやみつきになります。まずは、ショート落語からチャレンジです。

《Short Rakugo : Monkey From Taiwan》

◆A man goes into a pet shop.
【A】May I help you, sir?
【B】Do you have any rare animals for pets?
【A】Yeah, we do. We have monkeys from Taiwan. We sell them in sets of five.
【B】O.K. I'll take a set.
【A】Thank you, sir.
◆The next day, the man comes back to the pet shop and complains.
【B】B: Hey, man! You said these monkeys were from Taiwan, but I found one that was a Japanese monkey.
【A】Oh, that one's the interpreter, sir.

《ショート落語：台湾から来た猿》

◆ある男がペットショップにやって来て、
【A】今日は何がご入用で。
【B】おまはんとこ、なんかめずらしいペットあるか。
【A】へえ、おまっせ。ちょうど台湾から来ためずらしい猿がおまっせ。5匹セットで買うてもらわなあきませんけどな。（英語では「ちょうど」や「めずらしい」が入ってないが、気分的には入れて下さい。）
【B】かまへん。それもらうわ。
【A】おおきに。
◆そやけどその男、次の日に文句言いに来よって。
【B】こら。おっちゃん。こいつら台湾から来た言うたけど、一匹日本猿がまじってるやんか。
【A】ああ、それ、通訳ですねん。

おわりに

今井 恒雄（Tsuneo Imai）

　高座で英語落語を語るなんて、素人が出来るはずはないと思うでしょう。でも、大阪の「ＨＯＥインターナショナル」という英語学校では、山本正昭氏の指導の下、生徒さん達は、長年、英語落語に励んでおり、テレビにも出演しています。私達も、その教室で落語を演じるＡＢＣを学びました。

　本書では落語のスタイルを使って、日本語と英語で、新作落語や、水泳の流体力学についての落語を、楽しく読めるようにまとめました。

　これまでのシリーズを通した筆者らの願いは、読んだ後で何かを始める意欲を感じてもらうことです。始めれば何とかなります。一番重要なのは「頑張ること」と「繰り返すこと」だと信じています。

　著者の平木はこの考え方を貫き、長年、京都産業大学、東京家政学院筑波女子大学で若き学生の指導に当たってきました。著者の今井は、２００４年の１０月から、京都の大学院でコンピュータに関することを教えていますが、平木と同様に学生達にこの精神を身に付けて社会に出て欲しいと願っています。読者の皆様も、熱中し、頑張り、繰り返すことで、自分の立てた目標を実現させて下さい。

　また、何をするにしても、一人で出来る範囲は限られています。仕事も組織で進めるように、仕事以外でも仲間が大切です。本トロイカ・シリーズが続いたのも、著者らがそれぞれ個性と得意分野が違いながらも、ウマが合っていたからだと思っています。そうした仲間に恵まれた幸運に感謝しています。

　なお、本書のイラストは、Ⅳ [2]「ENGLISH RAKUGO」の部分を境山哲夫氏が、それ以外の部分を上原五百枝氏が担当しました。

　本書を出版するに当たり下記の方々にお世話になりました。

　イアン・ウイルソン氏、および、ＮＯＶＡアカデミーの先生方。翻訳の際には、多々、チェックをしていただき、ありがとうございました。

　本書の出版に当たり、㈱恒星社厚生閣の片岡一成氏に、今回も大変お世話になりました。

　皆さまのお陰で、本書が無事、出版出来ましたことを心から感謝致します。

In Closing...

Tsuneo Imai

Who can believe that an amateur can perform RAKUGO on stage, much less perform it in English. But, Mr.Masaaki Yamamoto has taught how to perform RAKUGO stories in English at an English conversation school named "HOE International" in Osaka for a long time. They have appeared on TV. several times. We also spent our grounding in how to perform rakugo in English at the "HOE International".

We hope that our readers will feel inspired to try something new, through the series that we have written. If you start, things will work out. We believe that "effort" and "repetition" are most important.

Shigeko Hiraki has lived up to these principles, and she has encouraged the students of "Kyoto Sangyo Univ." and "Tokyo Kasei Gakuin Tsukuba Women's Univ.". Tsuneo Imai has taught at a post graduate school in Kyoto since October 2004 and he has also desired to encourage his students to learn these ways of thinking before they graduate.

It is our wish that readers will realize thier own goal by "enthusiasm", "effort" and "repetition". Whatever you want to do, it's difficult to achieve a big result on your own. As you know, for a business to go forward, you willneed some good partners. We appreciate that each of us aregifted with nice partners to have written these books that are in the Troika series for such a long time together.

We each have different characters and specialities.

Mr.Sakaiyama drew the illustrations in Ⅳ [2] "English RAKUGO" and Ms.Uehara did all the others.

We appreciate the help of the many people involved in this publication.

Mr.Ian Wilson and other teachers at NOVA Academy. They assisted us in our translation to English.

We want to thank Mr.Kazunari Kataoka, Koseisya-Koseikaku Co. for his cooperation.

We wish, finally to thank you all for the publishing of the book.

トロイカ・ライブラリ／Troika Library

〈インターネット・英語関係〉

英語落語・日本語落語で生き生き人生！
Refresh Your Life Using Rakugo!

平木茂子・今井恒雄 編著
山本正昭・竹島良憲・山田悟史・上原五百枝・根尾延子 著
B5判／144頁／並製／本体1,500円
7699-1022-3 C1082／010-00021-00

《日英対訳／落語ドラマ》八つぁん・熊さんと一緒に、英語落語への挑戦、やさしい水泳の流体力学への挑戦をしてみませんか！

落語をつかって英語・日本語を学ぼう《日英 対訳》
英語落語・日本語落語 大集合！
A Big Selection Of Rakugo In English And Japanese!

平木茂子・今井恒雄 編著
上原五百枝・槇江延子・テーラー、マーク・バートン、ダーレン・マクアリア、マーク 著 上原五百枝 絵
B5判／172頁／並製／本体1,500円
7699-1002-9 C000／010-00020-00

《日英対訳／落語ドラマ》八つぁん・熊さんと一緒に、コンピュータの分かりにくい所を、やさしい説明で見直してみませんか！

三訂版
―八つぁん・熊さんと一緒に楽しむ―
誰にでも使えるインターネット

平木茂子 編著
今井恒雄・土屋富雄 著　上原五百枝 絵
B5判／96頁／並製／本体1,100円
7699-0863-6 C1055／010-00019-00

インターネットは楽しむもの。勉強なんて、いらなーい！八つぁん・熊さんと一緒に、これを体験しましょう！

―中高年者のために・知的障害者のために―
インターネット講習会を
開いてみませんか！

平木茂子 編著
今井恒雄・土屋富雄・廣澤美恵子 著　今井恒雄・譲原玉枝 絵
B5判／96頁／並製／本体1,100円
7699-0896-2 C1055／010-00016-00

「講習会はどうあるべきか？」を理解して、貴方も、インターネット講習会を計画してみませんか！

―中高年者・ろうあ者・知的障害者のために―
そのまま読めば，落伍をさせない
インターネット講習会！

平木茂子 編著
今井恒雄・土屋富雄・廣澤美恵子・金子源治 著　今井恒雄・譲原玉枝 絵
B5判／96頁／並製／本体1,100円
7699-0914-4 C1055／010-00017-00

《読み上げ原稿付き》読み上げ原稿というのをご存知ですか？講習会での説明が、原稿の形になっているので、貴方も、初級インターネット講習会を開くことが出来ます。

―小学生から高齢者まで―
英語でインターネット講習会を開いてみよう！
Let's Hold Internet Workshops In English!

平木茂子 編著
今井恒雄・ジュペ，R・バートン，D ほか 著
B5判／108頁／並製／本体1,280円
7699-0952-7 C1055／010-00018-00

《日英対訳／読み上げ原稿付き》自分達だけで、初級インターネット講習会を、英語、或いは、日本語で開いてみようという方々を対象にしています。英語の勉強にも最適です。

―英語がコワイと思っているアナタへ！―
英字新聞を読んでみよう！
Let's Read English-Language Newspapers!

平木茂子 編著
今井恒雄・バートン，D・マクアリア，M ほか 著
B5判／108頁／並製／本体1,280円
7699-0965-9 C1089／010-00020-00

《日英対訳》英字新聞を読んでみたいと思ったことはありませんか？初級の英語の知識さえあれば、誰でも英字新聞を楽しめます！

―やってみようよ、いつまでも！―
英会話、ついでに英語の読み・書きも！
Let's Practice all 4 English Skills Together!

平木茂子 編著
今井恒雄・バートン、ダーレン・根尾延子・岡田真二 著
B5判／86頁／並製／本体1,280円
7699-0982-9 C1082／010-00021-00

《日英対訳／フリガナ付き》「英会話、大好き！」という人はいっぱいいます。読み・書きも一緒にやって効果を上げてみませんか！問題形式で解答つき。初級用。

〈システム設計・OA化・COBOL言語関係〉

落語でわかるOA化
―八つぁん熊さん奮闘記―

平木茂子 著　今井恒雄 編　上原五百枝 絵
A5判/386頁/並製/本体3,000円
7699-0753-2 C1055/010-00003-00

《落語ドラマ》八つぁん・熊さんと一緒に、コンピュータとは？ OA化とは？ を、もう一度考え直してみませんか！ これまでの考えとは逆であることに気づくと思います。コンピュータの知識がゼロの方、これさえ読めば「なーんだ、そうだったのか！」

システム設計入門
―誰にでも出来るOA化―

平木茂子・今井恒雄・荒木雄豪 著　渡辺末美 絵
A5判/386頁/並製/本体3,000円
7699-0753-2 C1055/010-00003-00

システム設計って、難しいと思っていませんか？「今月は食費を節約して家族旅行に行こう」を考えるのもシステム設計。この本の問題をこなしたら、ホーラ、貴方もシステム設計者！（問題数：107　解答例つき）

自分でやろうOA化
―算盤並のコンピューター

平木茂子・今井恒雄・荒木雄豪 著　上原五百枝 絵
A5判/390頁/並製/本体3,200円
7699-0828-8 C1055/010-00011-00

手作業でやっている仕事のOA化を、外注に頼る企業は多いと思います。しかし、OA化は仕事をよく知っている現場の人が行うのが最高！「どうして」ですって？ まぁ、とにかく、読んでみて下さい！

ファイル処理入門―COBOLの文法―
―算盤並のコンピューター

平木茂子・荒木雄豪・今井恒雄 著
A5判/514頁/並製/本体3,690円
7699-0677-3 C1055/010-00006-00

OA化の基礎となるCOBOL言語の文法・ファイルの作成・フローチャート・初級システム設計を、この本の問題を解きながら頭に入れましょう！ コンピュータの知識がなくてもOK。クイズのつもりで、さぁスタート！（問題数：187　解答例つき）

PFD入門―FACOM大型機ユーザーのために―
―算盤並のコンピューター

今井恒雄・荒木雄豪・平木茂子 著
A5判/176頁/並製/本体1,750円
7699-0683-8 C1055/010-00005-00

コンピュータ、および、エディタ（PFD）の使用方法が問題形式になっているので、楽しく簡単に覚えられます！（問題数：39　解答例つき）

COBOLによる業務プログラムの作成〔Ⅰ〕
―算盤並のコンピューター

平木茂子 著
A5判/並製/198頁/本体2,650円
7699-0652-8 C1055/010-00001-00

やさしいプログラム、帳票作成プログラムをいっぱい作ります。これで貴方はOA化での帳票作成プログラマ！（問題数：92　解答例つき）

COBOLによる業務プログラムの作成〔Ⅱ〕
―算盤並のコンピューター

平木茂子 著
A5判/並製/230頁/本体3,650円
7699-0654-4 C1055/010-00002-00

帳票作成プログラムが作れるようになったら、この本の問題を通して、テーブル処理・サブルーチン・色々な形の業務プログラムにチャレンジしましょう。ここまでやれば、どんなプログラムも怖くない！（問題数：79　解答例つき）

〈水泳の流体力学関係〉

楽しい・水泳の流体力学
―コーチ・選手・中高年スイマーのための―

平木茂子 編
竹島良憲・今井恒雄 ほか 著　見一真理子 絵
A5判/290頁/並製/本体2,000円
7699-0781-8 C0075/003-00019-00

飛び込む時、どうしてゴーグルは外れるのか？ どうしたら外れなくなるのか？ こんな疑問にお答えします！

生活の中の楽しい水泳《品切れ》
―やさしい流体力学を覚えよう―

平木茂子 編著
今井恒雄・竹島良憲・加藤和春・内山峰樹 著　上原五百枝ほか 絵
B5判/166頁/並製/本体1,500円
7699-0868-7 C0075/003-00021-00

ホンのちょっとの流体力学の知識があれば、貴方のタイムはグーンとアップ

（株）恒星社厚生閣　TEL：03-3359-7371、FAX：03-3359-7375
Eメール：sales@kouseisha.com、ホームページ：http://www.kouseisha.com/

| チーム紹介：五十音順／Introducing The Team : Japanese alphabetical order |

- ◆ 今井 恒雄：京都情報大学院大学・教授（日本）
- ◇ Imai Tsuneo : Professor of The Kyoto College of Graduate Studies for Informatics (Japan)
- ◆ 上原 五百枝：イラストレーター（日本）
- ◇ Uehara Ioe : Illustrator (Japan)
- ◆ 境山 哲夫：イラストレーター（日本）
- ◇ Sakaiyama Tetsuo : Illustrator (Japan)
- ◆ 竹島 良憲：川崎重工業株式会社・航空宇宙カンパニー技術企画管理部（日本）
- ◇ Takeshima Yoshinori : Engineering Division, Aerospace Company, Kawasaki Heavy Industries, Ltd (Japan)
- ◆ テーラー、マーク：英語教師（オーストラリア）
- ◇ Taylor, Mark : English teacher (Australia)
- ◆ 根尾 延子：主婦（日本）
- ◇ Neo Nobuko : House wife (Japan)
- ◆ 平木 茂子：作家（日本）
- ◇ Hiraki Shigeko : Writer (Japan)
- ◆ マクアリア、マーク：英語教師（カナダ）
- ◇ McAlear, Mark : English teacher (Canada)
- ◆ 山田 悟史：ＮＰＯ法人スポーツ・ソリューション代表
- ◇ Yamada Satoshi : President of Sport Solution (A non-profit organization) (Japan)
- ◆ 山本 正昭：ＨＯＥインターナショナル代表（日本）
- ◇ Yamamoto Masaaki : Director of HOE International (Japan)

１９６９年、英会話学校「ＨＯＥ」を大阪のビジネス街、淀屋橋に設立。１９８３年に「爆笑王」の名を持つ落語家、桂枝雀さんが英会話を習いに来られ、英語落語が誕生。国内はもとより、海外公演も数多く企画し、著者自身も舞台に立ち、ＭＣや、また、桂雀枝さんとも共演。その他、ビル・クラウリ、桂かい枝、ダイアン吉日など、多くの演者を生み出し、また現在は、英語落語道場を開き、演者の育成に当たっている。

【nb : Family names are listed first, as is usual in Japan. 】

本書の情報は、下のホームページアドレスで
ご覧下さい。
（http://www.kasei.ac.jp/cs/sh/）

版権所有
検印省略

《日・英対訳／In Japanese & English》

英語落語・日本語落語で生き生き人生！
Refresh Your Life Using Rakugo!

平成17年8月1日　初版1刷発行	平木茂子・今井恒雄（編・著） 山本正昭・竹島良憲・山田悟史・ 上原五百枝・根尾延子・ テーラー、マーク・マクアリア、マーク

発行者　片岡　一成
印刷所　協友印刷有限会社
製本所　協栄製本株式会社
発行所／㈱恒星社厚生閣
〒160-0008　東京都新宿区三栄町8

TEL　03(3359)7371(代)
FAX　03(3359)7375
http://www.kouseisha.com/

（定価はカバーに表示）

Ⓒ S. HIRAKI, T. IMAI　Printed in Japan, 2005

ISBN4-7699-1022-3　C1082